ANDREW DAVIS

AI Gold Rush

Proven Methods to Make Money with Artificial Intelligence

Contents

Introduction

Welcome to the Gold Rush

Welcome to an era defined by rapid innovation and boundless opportunity. Today, we stand at the crossroads of a technological revolution—an AI revolution—that is reshaping the world of business, creativity, and everyday life. In many ways, this moment is as transformative as the historical gold rushes and Industrial Revolutions that have punctuated human history. Just as prospectors once flocked to new frontiers in search of fortune, innovators and entrepreneurs are now venturing into the expansive landscape of artificial intelligence, ready to stake their claim on a digital gold mine.

In this introduction, we'll explore why this moment matters, draw parallels between today's AI surge and past transformative eras, and outline who will benefit most from the insights in this book. We'll also provide a roadmap for how to use this guide to pick a lane, experiment, and scale your efforts to generate meaningful income.

The AI Revolution: Why This Moment Matters

Artificial intelligence is no longer a futuristic concept relegated to science fiction; it is a tangible force that is changing the very fabric of our society. What makes this moment unique is the rapid pace of technological advancements and the increasing accessibility of AI tools. In decades past, breakthroughs in technology were confined to well-funded research labs and large corporations. Today, AI-powered platforms and applications are available to anyone with an internet connection. This democratization of technology means that individuals, regardless of their background or resources, can harness AI to create value, solve problems, and generate income.

The AI revolution matters because it levels the playing field. It enables small businesses, freelancers, and side hustlers to compete with larger entities by automating tasks, analyzing data, and generating creative content at a fraction of the traditional cost. With AI, what once took months of labor can now be accomplished in days, or even hours. This efficiency doesn't just boost productivity—it also opens the door to entirely new business models and revenue streams that were unimaginable just a few years ago.

Moreover, the implications of AI extend beyond just efficiency. AI technologies are now being used to personalize customer experiences, predict market trends, and optimize complex processes. This convergence of technological capability and creative potential means that the traditional boundaries of industries are being redrawn. The opportunities emerging from this AI revolution are not just incremental improvements; they are exponential in their potential impact, offering unprecedented possibilities for those willing to explore and innovate.

Comparing AI to Historical Gold Rushes and Technological Revolutions

To truly appreciate the magnitude of what we're experiencing today, it helps to look back at historical events that reshaped societies and economies. The gold rushes of the 19th century serve as a powerful metaphor for today's AI landscape. During those times, thousands of people rushed to uncharted territories with the hope of striking it rich. These events were characterized by high risks, rapid changes, and the potential for enormous rewards. Similarly, the AI revolution presents both challenges and significant opportunities. Instead of searching for literal gold, today's pioneers are mining data and harnessing computational power to create wealth and drive innovation.

Like the Industrial Revolution, which fundamentally changed how we produce goods and live our lives, AI is redefining our relationship with work and technology. The Industrial Revolution brought about the mechanization of labor, leading to increased productivity and the creation of entirely new industries. AI is doing much the same by automating repetitive tasks, enabling advanced analytics, and facilitating new forms of creativity. But beyond automation, AI offers something even more transformative: the ability to learn, adapt, and improve over time. This dynamic quality means that AI isn't just a static tool; it's an evolving partner that can help you solve problems

3

in ways that were previously impossible.

In historical gold rushes, the promise of quick riches often led to a frenzy of activity and competition. Today's AI landscape is similarly competitive, yet it is also collaborative. The open-source nature of many AI tools means that breakthroughs and innovations are shared rapidly across the global community. This collaborative spirit accelerates progress and democratizes access to technology, ensuring that the benefits of AI can be enjoyed by a broader audience than ever before.

Who This Book Is For

The insights contained within this book are designed to be accessible and actionable for a diverse audience. Whether you are a freelancer, a side hustler, a business owner, or a creative, the strategies presented here can help you leverage AI to generate income and drive growth.

- **Freelancers:** If you're an independent professional looking to boost your productivity and expand your service offerings, this book will introduce you to AI tools that can automate routine tasks, enhance your creativity, and help you deliver exceptional results to your clients.
- **Side Hustlers:** For those juggling a full-time job or other commitments, the AI revolution offers a pathway to explore new revenue streams with minimal initial investment. This book provides practical methods to test ideas on a small scale, refine your approach, and eventually scale your

efforts into a sustainable income source.

- **Business Owners:** Whether you run a small business or a growing startup, integrating AI into your operations can be a game changer. The strategies in this book will help you identify areas where AI can streamline processes, improve customer engagement, and provide a competitive edge in your industry.
- **Creators:** Artists, writers, marketers, and digital content producers will find a wealth of inspiration in these pages. AI isn't just a tool for efficiency—it's a partner in creativity. Learn how to use AI to generate innovative ideas, create compelling content, and engage audiences in new and exciting ways.

The beauty of AI lies in its versatility. No matter your current skill set or background, the tools and strategies discussed in this book are designed to be adaptable, ensuring that you can find a method that fits your unique circumstances and goals.

What You'll Get Out of This Book

Inside "AI Gold Rush," you will find a comprehensive guide that demystifies the process of using AI to create revenue streams. The book is structured to offer a blend of theoretical insights, practical advice, and real-world examples that illustrate the power of AI in action.

Here's what you can expect:

- **In-Depth Understanding of AI Tools and Technologies:** Gain clarity on what artificial intelligence is, how it works, and why it's a game changer. We break down complex concepts into easy-to-understand language, ensuring that you can confidently navigate the AI landscape.
- **Practical Strategies for Different Income Streams:** Explore a range of methods to leverage AI for profit. Whether it's freelancing, content creation, e-commerce, or consulting, you'll find detailed strategies tailored to various avenues of revenue generation.
- **Actionable Case Studies and Success Stories:** Learn from those who have already paved the way. Through case studies and real-life examples, you'll see how individuals and businesses have successfully implemented AI strategies to transform their financial lives.
- **Step-by-Step Guides:** Each chapter includes detailed, actionable steps to help you implement AI strategies in your own projects. From initial concept to full-scale execution, you'll have a roadmap to follow that minimizes risk and maximizes potential returns.
- **Tools, Templates, and Resources:** Benefit from curated lists of AI tools, practical templates, and resource directories that will accelerate your journey. These resources are designed to help you get started quickly and scale your efforts as you gain momentum.
- **A Mindset Shift:** Perhaps most importantly, this book is designed to inspire a shift in perspective. Embrace the entrepreneurial mindset required to succeed in an AI-driven world. Learn to view challenges as opportunities and to continually innovate in the face of rapid technological change.

By the end of this book, you will not only have a robust understanding of the current AI landscape but also a practical plan for tapping into its potential. Whether you're looking to build a side hustle or scale an existing venture, you'll have the tools and insights necessary to succeed.

How to Use This Book: Pick a Lane, Experiment, and Scale

Success in the AI-driven economy is not about following a single, rigid formula—it's about finding the path that aligns best with your skills, interests, and goals. This book is organized into distinct "lanes" or methods, each representing a different way to leverage AI for income generation. Here's how to make the most of this guide:

- **Pick a Lane:** As you begin, review the different approaches presented throughout the book. Identify the lanes that resonate most with you. Are you drawn to freelancing, where AI can help streamline your work and boost productivity? Or are you more interested in content creation, using AI to generate engaging videos, blogs, or social media posts? Perhaps e-commerce or consulting piques your interest. Choose one or two lanes that align with your current abilities and aspirations.
- **Experiment:** Once you've selected your lane, start small. Use the actionable strategies and step-by-step guides in this book to test out your ideas on a manageable scale. Experimentation is crucial in the world of AI—technology

7

is evolving rapidly, and what works today might need tweaking tomorrow. Embrace a mindset of continuous learning. Allow yourself the freedom to fail, iterate, and refine your approach based on real-world feedback and results.

- **Scale:** After you've validated your concept through experimentation, it's time to scale. This book provides scaling strategies designed to help you expand your efforts without overwhelming your resources. Learn how to automate repetitive tasks, delegate where possible, and reinvest your gains to grow your venture sustainably. Scaling isn't just about increasing revenue—it's about building a robust, resilient operation that can adapt to the dynamic AI landscape.

Throughout this journey, remember that the AI revolution is as much about mindset as it is about technology. The willingness to adapt, experiment, and continuously improve is what will set you apart. Use this book as a roadmap, but also as a source of inspiration. The strategies detailed in the chapters that follow are not prescriptive formulas—they're starting points meant to ignite your creativity and propel you toward success.

As you navigate through this guide, keep an eye out for practical tips, detailed case studies, and expert insights that can help you make informed decisions. This is your toolkit for thriving in an era where technology and innovation are your greatest assets. The gold rush is on, and the tools to mine your fortune are at your fingertips. Embrace the opportunities that lie ahead, and get ready to transform your ideas into reality.

In the pages that follow, we will explore a range of proven methods to harness AI for financial success. Whether you're aiming to build a profitable side hustle, grow your existing business, or launch a new venture, the insights in this book are designed to guide you every step of the way. Welcome to the AI Gold Rush—your journey toward innovation, growth, and prosperity starts now.

By diving deep into the possibilities of artificial intelligence and understanding how it can be applied across various domains, you'll be equipped to navigate the challenges and seize the opportunities of this dynamic landscape. Prepare to embark on a journey that will not only reshape the way you think about work and technology but also redefine your path to financial freedom.

Let's begin this exploration into the transformative power of AI. The road ahead is filled with promise, and with the right mindset and tools, you can tap into the immense potential of this technological gold mine. Welcome to the future. Welcome to the Gold Rush.

1

Chapter 1: The Foundations of AI Money-Making

In today's rapidly evolving digital economy, artificial intelligence is emerging as one of the most transformative forces, reshaping the way businesses operate, products are created, and opportunities are seized. This chapter lays the groundwork for understanding AI and its potential as a tool for generating income. We will explore what AI truly is—stripped of overly technical jargon—examine the various categories of AI tools, discuss the essential mindset shift from being a consumer of technology to becoming a creator and innovator, and consider the risks, ethics, and opportunities that come with embracing AI.

Understanding What AI Really Is

At its most basic, artificial intelligence refers to the capability of machines to perform tasks that typically require human intelligence. These tasks can include understanding language, recognizing patterns, solving problems, and even learning from experience. Imagine having a digital assistant that doesn't just follow a fixed set of instructions but can adapt its behavior based on new data—this is the promise of AI.

AI is not a mystical or magical force; it is built on algorithms and data. These algorithms are sets of rules and procedures that computers use to process information and make decisions. When combined with vast amounts of data, these systems can "learn" by finding patterns and improving their performance over time. This process, often called machine learning, is at the heart of what makes AI both powerful and versatile.

Importantly, AI isn't about replacing human ingenuity but augmenting it. It can take over repetitive tasks, analyze complex data sets at high speed, and generate creative content, thereby freeing up human beings to focus on higher-level strategic thinking, innovation, and interpersonal engagement. By viewing AI as a collaborator rather than a competitor, you can unlock new ways to generate income and add value to your projects.

Categories of AI Tools

AI tools can be broadly categorized into three main groups: generative, predictive, and automation. Each of these categories offers unique capabilities that can be harnessed for different aspects of money-making ventures.

Generative AI

Generative AI is the branch of artificial intelligence that creates new content, whether it be text, images, music, or even video. This type of AI is particularly useful for content creators and digital marketers, as it can help generate ideas, write articles, design graphics, and produce multimedia content. Some key characteristics of generative AI include:

- **Creativity on Demand**: With generative AI, you can quickly produce a wide array of content based on specific inputs or prompts. This ability enables you to experiment with different styles and formats without having to start from scratch every time.
- **Speed and Scale:** What might take hours or days for a human to produce can often be accomplished in minutes with generative AI tools. This speed is especially beneficial when you need to create content in bulk or meet tight deadlines.
- **Customization**: Many generative AI systems allow you to tailor the output to your specific needs, whether it's the tone of a marketing campaign or the design of a product. This level of customization can help ensure that your content stands out in a crowded marketplace.

By leveraging generative AI, freelancers, marketers, and entrepreneurs can significantly reduce the time and cost associated with content creation, enabling them to focus on strategic growth and customer engagement.

Predictive AI

Predictive AI, as the name suggests, is designed to forecast outcomes based on historical data. It uses statistical models and machine learning techniques to analyze past trends and predict future events. This category of AI is invaluable for decision-making in various sectors such as finance, marketing, and operations. Key aspects of predictive AI include:

- **Data-Driven Insights**: Predictive tools analyze large volumes of data to identify trends, patterns, and correlations that may not be immediately obvious to human analysts. This helps businesses make more informed decisions.
- **Risk Mitigation**: By forecasting potential risks or market shifts, predictive AI can help you anticipate challenges before they become critical issues, allowing you to take proactive measures.
- **Personalization**: In marketing and customer service, predictive AI can be used to anticipate customer needs and tailor experiences accordingly. This can lead to higher customer satisfaction and retention rates.

For those looking to generate income, predictive AI can be harnessed to optimize marketing strategies, manage investments, or even design better products by anticipating market trends and consumer behavior.

Automation AI

Automation AI is about streamlining and optimizing repetitive tasks. By automating routine processes, businesses can operate more efficiently and at a lower cost. Automation AI encompasses tools that manage everything from customer service interactions and data entry to complex supply chain logistics. The primary benefits include:

- **Efficiency and Consistenc**y: Automation ensures that tasks are performed consistently and without the human errors that can occur with manual processing. This is crucial for maintaining high standards in business operations.
- **Scalability**: With automated processes, it's easier to scale operations without a proportional increase in labor costs. This scalability is vital for growing businesses that need to manage higher volumes of work.
- **Focus on Strategic Tasks**: When routine tasks are automated, you and your team can focus on strategic, high-value activities that drive growth and innovation.

Automation AI is especially useful for entrepreneurs and business owners who want to streamline their operations, reduce overhead, and free up resources to focus on expanding their ventures.

The Mindset Shift: From Consumer to Creator with AI

One of the most significant shifts brought about by the AI revolution is the move from being a passive consumer of technology to becoming an active creator and innovator. Historically, most people have interacted with technology in a consumer capacity—using tools and applications designed by others. However, AI is democratizing creation in a way that was previously unimaginable.

Embracing the Role of a Creator

Today, AI is empowering individuals to become creators rather than just users. With the advent of user-friendly AI tools, anyone can produce high-quality content, develop innovative products, or build robust business models. This democratization means that you no longer need a team of specialists or a large budget to create something valuable. Instead, you can use AI to:

- **Generate Content**: Whether it's writing articles, composing music, or designing visuals, AI can help you produce creative work that meets professional standards.
- **Develop Products**: AI tools can assist in everything from product design and prototyping to testing and market analysis. This enables you to bring innovative products to market faster.
- **Solve Complex Problems**: With AI's ability to process and analyze large data sets, you can tackle challenges that were previously too complex or time-consuming to solve manually.

Shifting Your Perspective

The transformation from consumer to creator requires a change in mindset. Instead of passively using technology, you must learn to see it as a tool for innovation and growth. Here are some ways to make that shift:

- **Invest in Learning**: Embrace continuous learning. Explore courses, tutorials, and communities that focus on AI and its applications. The more you understand about the technology, the more effectively you can harness its power.
- **Experiment Without Fear**: AI is a field of experimentation. Don't be afraid to try new tools and approaches—even if they don't work perfectly at first. Each experiment is a learning opportunity that can guide you toward success.
- **Value Creativity Over Perfection**: The goal is not to produce perfect work but to create something that adds value. Use AI as a partner in your creative process, iterating and refining your output over time.
- **Embrace Failure as a Stepping Stone**: Not every experiment will be a success. View failures as valuable lessons that bring you closer to innovative solutions. This resilience is key to thriving in an AI-driven world.

By shifting your mindset from that of a passive user to an active creator, you open up a world of possibilities. You start to see challenges as opportunities and gaps in the market as potential avenues for innovation. This perspective not only fuels creativity but also positions you to take full advantage of the economic opportunities that AI presents.

Risks, Ethics, and Opportunities

While the potential of AI is immense, it's crucial to understand that it comes with its own set of risks and ethical considerations. A balanced approach to adopting AI means being aware of these challenges and addressing them proactively.

Recognizing the Risks

As with any powerful technology, there are risks associated with AI:

- **Job Displacement:** One of the most discussed risks is the potential for AI to automate jobs traditionally performed by humans. While automation can lead to increased efficiency, it may also result in job losses in certain sectors. Being mindful of this risk means preparing to upskill and adapt to new roles that complement AI technologies.
- **Data Privacy and Security**: AI systems often rely on large datasets, some of which may include sensitive personal or business information. Ensuring that data is handled responsibly and securely is critical to maintaining trust and complying with legal requirements.
- **Bias and Fairness**: AI systems are only as good as the data they are trained on. If the data is biased or incomplete, the AI's output may reflect those biases, leading to unfair or discriminatory outcomes. Recognizing this risk encourages the development and use of more robust, unbiased data sets and algorithms.

17

- **Over-Reliance on Automation**: While AI can streamline many processes, an over-reliance on automation may lead to a loss of critical human oversight. It is essential to strike a balance between leveraging AI's capabilities and maintaining human judgment and creativity in decision-making processes.

Navigating Ethical Considerations

Ethics play a crucial role in the development and deployment of AI. As you explore ways to make money with AI, consider these ethical principles:

- **Transparency**: Be open about when and how AI is being used in your projects. Transparency builds trust with customers, partners, and stakeholders.
- **Accountability**: Ensure that there is accountability in the use of AI systems. When errors or biases occur, having clear protocols in place to address them is key.
- **Fairness**: Strive to create AI applications that treat all users equitably. This means actively working to identify and mitigate any biases in your data or algorithms.
- **Privacy**: Respect and protect the privacy of individuals. This involves not only adhering to legal standards but also following best practices in data management and security.
- **Social Responsibility**: Consider the broader societal impacts of your AI-driven initiatives. Aim to contribute positively to your community and industry rather than exacerbating inequalities or ethical dilemmas.

By keeping ethical considerations at the forefront of your endeavors, you can build trust and credibility—critical elements for long-term success in any business venture.

Seizing the Opportunities

The opportunities offered by AI far outweigh the challenges when approached with a thoughtful, balanced strategy. Here are some ways to capitalize on the potential of AI while mitigating its risks:

- **Innovative Business Models**: AI enables the creation of entirely new business models that were previously unfeasible. From subscription-based platforms to personalized services driven by predictive analytics, there is no shortage of innovative ways to generate revenue.
- **Cost Reduction and Efficiency**: Automation tools powered by AI can significantly lower operational costs by streamlining processes, reducing errors, and speeding up production. This increased efficiency can be reinvested in growing your business.
- **Enhanced Decision-Making**: Predictive AI tools can provide valuable insights that lead to better, data-driven decision-making. This capability is a boon for marketing strategies, investment decisions, and product development, giving you a competitive edge.
- **Scalability**: With the help of AI, scaling your business becomes more manageable. Automated systems can handle increased workloads without a corresponding increase in labor costs, making it easier to grow your venture sustainably.
- **Customization and Personalization**: AI-driven insights

allow you to tailor products and services to meet individual customer needs. This level of personalization can lead to higher customer satisfaction, loyalty, and ultimately, greater revenue.

- **Global Reach**: The accessibility of AI tools means that entrepreneurs and creators can reach a global audience without needing vast resources. Whether you're creating content, developing a product, or offering consulting services, AI levels the playing field and enables you to compete on a global scale.

The key to seizing these opportunities is a balanced, ethical approach. By understanding the inherent risks and taking proactive steps to address them, you can harness the power of AI responsibly and effectively. It's about blending innovation with caution—pioneering new methods to generate income while ensuring that your practices are sustainable, ethical, and in tune with the broader societal good.

Bringing It All Together

As we conclude this foundational chapter, it's clear that artificial intelligence is not just a fleeting trend; it is a robust and transformative tool that can redefine how we create value and generate income. The journey begins with a deep understanding of what AI really is—a collection of powerful tools designed to enhance human creativity, improve decision-making, and automate routine tasks. Whether it's through generating innovative content, predicting market trends, or streamlining business operations, AI offers myriad opportunities for those willing to embrace it.

However, the road to success with AI is not without challenges. It requires a fundamental mindset shift: transitioning from a passive consumer of technology to an active creator and innovator. This shift means investing in learning, being unafraid to experiment, and always striving for continuous improvement. At the same time, it necessitates a commitment to ethical practices—ensuring transparency, fairness, and accountability as you leverage AI's capabilities.

For entrepreneurs, freelancers, and side hustlers, the foundational principles discussed in this chapter are not just theoretical concepts but practical tools that can be applied to create sustainable, scalable income streams. The insights into the different categories of AI—generative, predictive, and automation—provide a roadmap for understanding how to apply these technologies in various contexts. Each category offers distinct benefits and can be integrated into your projects to maximize efficiency, creativity, and profitability.

As you move forward in your AI journey, remember that the true power of these technologies lies in your ability to harness them as part of a broader strategy. Use the tools at your disposal to experiment boldly, iterate rapidly, and scale intelligently. The AI revolution is a call to action—a chance to redefine what's possible in the world of work and entrepreneurship.

In the following chapters, we will dive deeper into each method of generating income with AI, offering practical strategies, case studies, and step-by-step guides to help you build your own ventures. Whether you are just beginning your exploration of AI or looking to enhance your existing efforts, the foundational insights shared here will serve as a solid base from which to launch your endeavors.

Embrace the potential of AI not just as a technological tool but as a catalyst for personal and professional transformation. The future of money-making is intertwined with the evolution of AI, and by laying a strong foundation today, you are positioning yourself at the forefront of tomorrow's opportunities. The journey from understanding AI to mastering it is both challenging and exhilarating—welcome to the start of a revolution that promises to reshape the landscape of income generation and innovation.

With this foundational knowledge in place, you are now ready to explore the myriad ways in which AI can be used to create wealth. The chapter ahead will break down actionable strategies that leverage these core concepts, guiding you step-by-step through the process of turning AI into a reliable source of income. Welcome to the future of entrepreneurship—welcome to the AI Gold Rush.

2

Chapter 2: Freelancing with AI Tools

The digital economy has leveled the playing field for freelancers, turning what was once a one-person operation into a fully functional agency. With the advent of powerful AI tools, you can now handle tasks that previously required large teams. In this chapter, we'll explore how you can build a one-person agency using AI, leverage top productivity tools like ChatGPT, Jasper, Canva, Grammarly, and Notion AI, offer a range of valuable services, find work on platforms like Upwork, Fiverr, and Contra, and learn from a case study of a freelancer who scaled from $0 to $5K per month with the help of AI.

Becoming a One-Person Agency Using AI

Imagine running a business where you control every aspect of operations, from ideation to execution, without the overhead of employees. This isn't a dream—it's the reality for many freelancers who harness AI. By using these tools, you can streamline your workflow, reduce costs, and deliver high-quality work that rivals larger agencies.

The Modern Freelancer's Advantage

AI tools act as digital team members that never sleep. They can produce content, optimize workflows, analyze data, and even generate creative ideas. This means that with a smart combination of these tools, a solo freelancer can handle multiple roles:

- **Content Creator**: Writing blog posts, social media updates, or marketing copy.
- **Designer**: Creating graphics, presentations, or visual content.
- **Researcher**: Gathering data and insights to drive strategic decisions.
- **Project Manager**: Organizing tasks and tracking progress with AI-powered project management tools.

In essence, AI empowers you to become a one-person agency, where you can provide a suite of services under one roof. This not only increases your potential revenue but also enhances your marketability as a versatile professional.

Tools to Enhance Productivity

To become an effective one-person agency, you need a robust set of tools that help you work faster and smarter. Here are some key AI tools that have proven indispensable for freelancers:

ChatGPT

ChatGPT is a conversational AI that can generate content, brainstorm ideas, and even help with customer communication. With its natural language processing capabilities, ChatGPT can assist in:

- Drafting emails, proposals, and project outlines.
- Creating initial drafts for articles or blog posts.
- Generating ideas for marketing campaigns or content topics.
- Answering client questions and providing customer support.

Its versatility makes it a powerful asset for any freelancer looking to streamline communication and content creation.

Jasper

Jasper is another AI writing assistant designed to help with creative content generation. It's particularly effective for:

- Writing compelling copy for websites, ads, and social media.
- Crafting long-form content such as eBooks or detailed

25

articles.
- Optimizing content for SEO by suggesting keywords and improving readability.
- Creating variations of content to test different marketing angles.

Jasper's ability to generate creative, persuasive content means you can produce high-quality work without spending excessive time on each project.

Canva

Canva is a graphic design tool that has integrated AI features to simplify the design process. It enables you to:

- Create stunning visuals for social media, presentations, and marketing materials.
- Use templates and AI-powered suggestions to enhance your designs.
- Collaborate on design projects with ease, even if you're not a professional designer.
- Customize graphics quickly to meet the specific needs of your clients.

By automating much of the design process, Canva allows you to deliver professional-quality visuals even if design isn't your core strength.

Grammarly

Grammarly is an AI-driven writing assistant focused on improving the quality of your text. It helps you to:

- Correct grammar, spelling, and punctuation errors.
- Enhance the clarity and style of your writing.
- Adapt your tone to fit different audiences and platforms.
- Ensure your content is professional and error-free.

Using Grammarly ensures that all your written communications—whether emails, reports, or social media posts—are polished and effective.

Notion AI

Notion AI builds on the capabilities of Notion, a popular productivity and organization tool. It assists you in:

- Organizing projects, tasks, and notes in one centralized location.
- Generating to-do lists, meeting notes, and project plans.
- Integrating various aspects of your workflow—from research to execution.
- Enhancing collaboration if you ever decide to bring in additional freelancers or partners.

Notion AI's ability to manage and streamline your work processes means you can focus more on delivering value to your clients and less on administrative overhead.

27

Services You Can Offer

With these AI tools at your disposal, your potential service offerings are expansive. Here's a look at some of the high-demand services you can provide:

Copywriting

High-quality copy is essential for any business, whether it's for websites, advertisements, or social media. Using AI, you can:

- Craft compelling headlines and persuasive body copy.
- Develop marketing content that resonates with target audiences.
- Write engaging email campaigns and sales letters.
- Optimize copy for SEO to drive organic traffic.

By integrating AI into your copywriting process, you can produce content faster and experiment with different tones and styles to see what works best.

Resume Writing and Professional Profiles

In today's competitive job market, a standout resume can make all the difference. AI can help you:

- Generate tailored resumes and cover letters for different industries.
- Optimize professional profiles on platforms like LinkedIn.

- Highlight key achievements and skills effectively.
- Ensure the language is concise, impactful, and error-free.

Offering resume writing services positions you as a critical partner for job seekers, career changers, and professionals looking to advance their careers.

Content Creation

Content is the backbone of digital marketing, and businesses are constantly in need of fresh, engaging material. With AI, you can:

- Produce blog posts, articles, and newsletters.
- Develop scripts for video content or podcasts.
- Create engaging social media content and campaigns.
- Repurpose content across different channels to maximize reach.

AI accelerates the content creation process, allowing you to maintain a steady output that keeps your clients' audiences engaged.

Research and Data Analysis

Every business decision is underpinned by good research. AI tools can streamline the research process by:

- Gathering and synthesizing information from various sources.
- Analyzing market trends and consumer behavior.

29

- Producing comprehensive reports and insights.
- Identifying opportunities and potential risks based on data.

By offering research services, you can help clients make informed decisions that drive growth and mitigate risk.

Platforms to Find Work

Finding clients is one of the most critical aspects of freelancing. Fortunately, several platforms cater specifically to freelancers and entrepreneurs looking to leverage their AI-enhanced skills. Here are some of the top platforms to consider:

Upwork

Upwork is one of the largest freelance marketplaces, connecting you with clients across a wide range of industries. On Upwork, you can:

- Create a detailed profile that highlights your AI-powered services.
- Bid on projects that align with your expertise.
- Build a portfolio showcasing your work and client testimonials.
- Utilize Upwork's messaging system to communicate directly with potential clients.

The platform's robust infrastructure and global reach make it an ideal starting point for freelancers looking to grow their business.

Fiverr

Fiverr offers a different model, where freelancers create "gigs" that outline specific services. On Fiverr, you can:

- Set up distinct service packages, from copywriting to graphic design.
- Define your pricing and delivery times upfront.
- Benefit from Fiverr's algorithm, which can help surface your services to potential clients.
- Gain exposure by receiving ratings and reviews that build your credibility.

Fiverr's user-friendly platform makes it easy to showcase your skills and attract clients looking for quick, reliable services.

Contra

Contra is a newer platform designed for independent creators and freelancers. It emphasizes long-term relationships and project-based work. On Contra, you can:

- Build a personal brand with a customizable profile that goes beyond a typical resume.
- Connect with companies and projects that value independent work.
- Showcase your portfolio and track record of successful projects.
- Engage with a community of like-minded professionals,

offering opportunities for collaboration and referrals.

Contra is particularly appealing if you're looking to establish a sustainable freelancing business that values quality and long-term partnerships over one-off gigs.

Case Study: From $0 to $5K/Month with AI Help

To illustrate the transformative power of AI for freelancers, consider the journey of Alex—a solo freelancer who leveraged AI tools to build a thriving one-person agency.

The Beginning

Alex started with little more than a laptop and a passion for writing. Recognizing that the competitive freelance landscape required more than just raw talent, Alex began exploring AI tools to enhance productivity. The goal was clear: maximize output without compromising on quality, and eventually, build a scalable business model.

Leveraging AI Tools

Content Generation with ChatGPT and Jasper:

- **Initial Projects**: Alex began by taking on small copywriting and content creation projects. Using ChatGPT, Alex generated first drafts for blog posts and marketing copy. Jasper was then used to refine the tone and add creative flair, ensuring that each piece was engaging and tailored to the client's brand.

- **Speed and Volume**: This dual-tool strategy allowed Alex to produce content at a pace that was previously unimaginable. Projects that once took days were now completed in hours, freeing up time to take on more work.

Design with Canva:

- **Creating Visual Content**: Realizing that clients increasingly demanded visually appealing content, Alex turned to Canva. Whether it was social media graphics, infographics, or presentations, Canva enabled Alex to create professional-quality visuals quickly.
- **Template Customization**: Leveraging AI-powered design suggestions and customizable templates, Alex built a library of design assets that could be quickly adapted to fit different client needs.

Polishing with Grammarly:

- **Error-Free Communication**: To ensure that every piece of content was polished and error-free, Alex integrated Grammarly into the workflow. This step was crucial in maintaining a high standard of quality across all written deliverables, from client emails to final project submissions.

Project Management with Notion AI:

- **Organizing Workflow**: With multiple projects and clients, staying organized was essential. Alex used Notion AI to manage projects, track deadlines, and store client briefs and feedback in one centralized place. This not only streamlined operations but also helped in planning for future growth.

Offering Diverse Services

Alex quickly realized that the true power of AI was in its versatility. Instead of limiting the services offered, Alex expanded into several high-demand areas:

- **Copywriting**: With the help of AI, Alex produced persuasive sales copy, detailed blog posts, and engaging social media content.
- **Resume and Profile Writing**: Recognizing a niche market, Alex began offering resume writing services. Using AI to optimize language and structure, Alex helped job seekers stand out in competitive markets.
- **Research and Data Analysis**: Leveraging AI's ability to synthesize information, Alex provided detailed market research reports that guided client strategies.
- **Design and Content Repurposing**: With Canva and Notion AI, Alex offered design services that complemented the written content, ensuring a cohesive brand experience for clients.

Finding Work on Freelance Platforms

To build a steady stream of clients, Alex leveraged platforms like Upwork, Fiverr, and Contra:

- **Upwork**: By crafting a detailed profile that highlighted the integration of AI tools, Alex attracted clients who were intrigued by the promise of fast, efficient, and high-quality work. Positive reviews and repeat business soon followed.
- **Fiverr**: On Fiverr, Alex created specialized gigs for each service offered, from copywriting to resume editing. The clear presentation and competitive pricing strategy helped gain traction quickly.
- **Contra**: Using Contra's emphasis on building a long-term professional brand, Alex secured several larger, project-based contracts. These relationships provided a steady income and valuable experience, further enhancing the portfolio.

Scaling Up

As word spread about Alex's efficiency and the quality of the work delivered, the freelancing business began to scale:

- **Increasing Rates**: With proven success and a robust portfolio, Alex was able to gradually increase rates. The combination of high output quality and rapid delivery justified premium pricing.
- **Diversifying Projects**: By continually expanding the range of services and targeting different niches—such as e-commerce content, technical writing, and creative storytelling—Alex diversified the income stream. This not only reduced dependency on a single type of work but also opened up opportunities in various markets.
- **Automation and Delegation**: Even as a one-person agency, Alex wasn't afraid to further integrate automation tools.

Routine tasks such as scheduling, invoicing, and even some basic customer inquiries were automated, freeing up even more time to focus on high-value projects.

The Outcome

Within a year, Alex's freelancing business had grown from sporadic gigs to a steady monthly income of $5,000. This achievement wasn't just about earning more—it was a transformation in how work was approached. By embracing AI, Alex managed to:

- Achieve a level of productivity that allowed for multiple projects concurrently.
- Maintain high quality, which led to excellent client retention and referrals.
- Develop a personal brand that stood out in a crowded marketplace.

Alex's journey is a testament to how a one-person agency can not only survive but thrive using AI. The key takeaway here is that AI tools aren't a replacement for human creativity or judgment—they're accelerators that amplify your capabilities, allowing you to deliver more value in less time.

Putting It All Together

The journey to becoming a successful freelancer in the AI era is both exciting and attainable. By leveraging AI tools like ChatGPT, Jasper, Canva, Grammarly, and Notion AI, you can create a one-person agency capable of handling a diverse array of services. The process involves:

- **Embracing the AI Advantage**: Recognize that AI can serve as your digital team member, handling repetitive tasks and enhancing creativity.
- **Investing in the Right Tools**: Equip yourself with tools that not only boost productivity but also ensure quality and consistency across all your deliverables.
- **Expanding Your Service Offerings**: Diversify your offerings—from copywriting and resume building to content creation and research—to appeal to a broader client base.
- **Utilizing Freelance Platforms**: Establish a presence on platforms like Upwork, Fiverr, and Contra to secure a steady stream of clients and build your reputation.
- **Learning from Success Stories**: Draw inspiration from freelancers like Alex, who used AI to scale from nothing to a thriving business generating thousands of dollars per month.

The modern freelancer has an unprecedented opportunity to not just participate in, but actively shape, the digital economy. With AI, you have the power to transform your work habits, deliver exceptional value, and create a business that scales with minimal overhead.

As you move forward, remember that the key to success lies in continuous learning and experimentation. The AI landscape is evolving rapidly, and staying up-to-date with the latest tools and trends will ensure you remain competitive. Whether you're just starting or looking to enhance your existing freelancing business, the integration of AI is not just an option—it's a necessity for thriving in today's fast-paced digital world.

In the following chapters, we will delve deeper into other methods to leverage AI for income generation. For now, focus on experimenting with these tools, refining your service offerings, and building a portfolio that showcases your ability to deliver high-quality work with the efficiency and precision that only AI can offer.

Embrace the potential of becoming a one-person agency. With dedication, smart use of AI tools, and a relentless focus on delivering value, you too can turn your freelance career into a scalable, profitable business. Welcome to the future of freelancing—where the right blend of technology and creativity can unlock extraordinary opportunities.

By integrating these strategies into your workflow, you not only streamline your operations but also build a brand that stands out in a competitive market. The journey may begin with small gigs, but with consistency, quality, and the powerful leverage of AI, you can scale your operations, command higher fees, and establish yourself as a trusted expert in your field.

Remember, every freelancer's journey is unique, but the principles remain the same: harness technology to work smarter, diversify your skills, and continuously adapt to the evolving digital landscape. As you apply these insights and tools, you will find yourself well on your way to building a sustainable, lucrative freelancing business in the age of AI.

This chapter serves as your blueprint for integrating AI into your freelance practice. Use it as a guide to unlock new possibilities, expand your offerings, and ultimately transform your career. The era of the one-person agency is here—armed with AI, you're ready to seize your share of the digital gold rush.

3

Chapter 3: AI-Powered Content Creation (YouTube, TikTok, Blogs)

The landscape of content creation is undergoing a revolution, thanks to artificial intelligence. What once required extensive planning, multiple specialized software, and long hours of editing can now be streamlined into a faster, more efficient process. With AI-powered tools, you can generate ideas, write scripts, edit videos, and even automate publishing. In this chapter, we will explore how to leverage AI for every step of the content creation process—from brainstorming to monetization—focusing on popular content types such as YouTube videos, TikTok clips, and blogs. We will also review top tools like Pictory, Descript, Runway ML, ChatGPT, and Midjourney, delve into various monetization paths, and outline strategies for niche content and consistent production. Finally, we'll provide a detailed example workflow from idea to upload.

Embracing AI in Content Creation

Content creation has always been about telling stories, sharing knowledge, and entertaining audiences. However, the time and expertise traditionally required to produce high-quality content can be daunting. AI offers a way to lower that barrier, enabling creators to focus on their unique voice and vision while letting technology handle the heavy lifting.

The AI Advantage

- **Speed and Efficiency:** AI tools can generate drafts, design visuals, and edit videos in a fraction of the time it would take manually.
- **Creativity Boost:** Using AI for ideation can spark creative ideas or provide alternative angles that you might not consider on your own.
- **Scalability:** With streamlined processes, it becomes easier to produce content on a regular basis, which is critical for building an audience.
- **Cost-Effectiveness:** Many AI tools are affordable and can replace multiple expensive software subscriptions, making high-quality production accessible on a tight budget.

By integrating AI into your workflow, you can maintain a consistent output while ensuring that every piece of content is polished and professional.

Using AI for Ideation, Scripting, Editing, and Publishing

Ideation

The journey begins with generating ideas. Brainstorming can be a slow process, especially when you need to produce content regularly. AI can accelerate this step by providing a wealth of suggestions and trends tailored to your niche.

- **ChatGPT:** Ask for ideas based on current trends, your target audience, or seasonal topics. For instance, you might ask, "What are some fresh content ideas for tech product reviews on YouTube?" ChatGPT can provide a list of topics complete with angles and questions to explore.
- **Midjourney:** Visual inspiration is a key part of ideation for many creators, especially if you're working on a visually driven platform like Instagram or TikTok. Midjourney can generate creative visuals or mood boards that help spark ideas for themes, color schemes, or video aesthetics.

Scripting

Once you've settled on an idea, the next step is developing a script. Scripts are the backbone of content, providing a structure and ensuring your message is clear.

- **ChatGPT & Jasper:** These tools can help you draft scripts for videos, blogs, or social media posts. By providing a brief outline or bullet points, you can get a full script draft that you can tweak to match your tone and style. For example, feeding ChatGPT a prompt like, "Write a 500-word script for a YouTube video on the latest smartphone trends," can quickly produce a draft that you can then personalize.

- **Notion AI:** If you use Notion for project management, Notion AI can help organize your ideas and transform outlines into detailed scripts, streamlining the writing process and ensuring you don't miss any key points.

Editing

Quality content requires editing—whether it's refining text, cutting video footage, or enhancing audio. AI-powered editing tools can significantly shorten the turnaround time from raw footage or rough drafts to polished products.

- **Descript:** This tool is particularly useful for video and audio editing. Descript offers features like automatic transcription, text-based editing, and even an overdub feature, allowing you to replace or edit spoken words without needing to re-record.
- **Pictory:** For those who produce video content, Pictory can convert long-form content into short, engaging clips. It analyzes video content, identifies key moments, and even adds captions and overlays. This is especially beneficial for repurposing long YouTube videos into shorter segments suitable for TikTok or Instagram.
- **Runway ML:** Runway ML brings advanced video editing capabilities by using AI to perform tasks such as background removal, color correction, and even style transfer. This tool is ideal for creators looking to add a professional polish to their videos without hiring an expert editor.

Publishing

Once your content is scripted, edited, and polished, the final step is publishing. AI can help schedule and optimize your posts to reach the right audience at the right time.

- **Social Media Management Tools:** Many social media management platforms now include AI features that analyze when your audience is most active and can automatically schedule your posts accordingly. This ensures you maintain a steady stream of content without having to manually manage every upload.
- **SEO Optimization:** For blog posts, AI-powered SEO tools can help optimize your content for search engines by suggesting keywords, meta descriptions, and readability improvements, ensuring your content performs well on platforms like Google.
- **Analytics:** Finally, AI-enhanced analytics tools can monitor performance across platforms, offering insights into what's working and providing data that you can use to refine your content strategy.

Top AI Tools for Content Creation

Let's take a deeper look at some of the most popular AI tools you can integrate into your content creation workflow.

Pictory

Pictory is a robust video editing tool that uses AI to simplify the process of creating engaging video content. It is designed to:

- **Convert long videos into short clips:** Identify highlights in long-form content and automatically create shorter, shareable segments.
- **Add captions and overlays:** Automatically generate captions and add branded overlays to make your videos more accessible and engaging.
- **Streamline video editing:** With an intuitive interface, even those with minimal editing experience can produce professional-looking videos.

Descript

Descript is a versatile tool for both audio and video editing, with an array of AI-driven features:

- **Automatic Transcription:** Transcribe your audio or video in real time, making the editing process more straightforward.
- **Text-Based Editing:** Edit your video or audio by editing the transcript, saving time and making precise edits easy.
- **Overdub Feature:** Replace words or add new lines without having to record additional audio.
- **Collaboration Tools:** Work seamlessly with team members or clients by sharing project files in the cloud.

Runway ML

Runway ML is an innovative platform that leverages machine learning for creative purposes:

- **Background Removal:** Remove or replace backgrounds in videos and images without the need for a green screen.
- **Style Transfer:** Apply artistic effects to your visuals, giving your content a unique look.
- **Real-Time Editing:** Make adjustments in real time, saving valuable post-production time.
- **Advanced Effects:** From color correction to object tracking, Runway ML offers a suite of tools that can elevate your video production quality.

ChatGPT

ChatGPT is an AI language model that assists in multiple areas of content creation:

- **Idea Generation:** Help brainstorm new topics, scripts, and blog post ideas tailored to your niche.
- **Drafting and Scripting:** Quickly create detailed scripts or outlines for videos, articles, or social media posts.
- **Editing Assistance:** Provide suggestions for improving tone, structure, and clarity.
- **Versatility:** Whether you're writing a blog post, video script, or social media caption, ChatGPT's flexible approach adapts to your creative needs.

Midjourney

Midjourney is an AI tool that inspires visual content creation:

- **Visual Ideation:** Generate digital artwork and mood boards to visually define your project's style.
- **Creative Concepting:** Use AI-generated imagery to explore different visual themes and aesthetic directions.
- **Integrative Design:** Supplement your video and blog content with unique, AI-crafted visual elements that enhance storytelling and brand consistency.

Monetization Paths for AI-Powered Content

Creating content is only half the battle; monetizing it effectively turns passion into profit. With the right strategy, you can generate revenue through multiple channels. Here are some key monetization paths:

Ad Revenue

- **YouTube Partner Program:** Monetize your videos by joining the YouTube Partner Program, where ad revenue is shared based on viewership.
- **Blog Ads:** Use platforms like Google AdSense to place ads on your blog. Consistent, high-quality content that attracts traffic can generate significant ad revenue.
- **Sponsored Content:** Work with brands to include sponsored messages or product placements in your videos or

blog posts. As your audience grows, these partnerships can become a substantial revenue source.

Affiliate Links

- **Product Reviews and Recommendations:** Integrate affiliate links into your content—whether in video descriptions or blog posts—to earn commissions on products you recommend.
- **Tutorials and How-To Guides:** Develop content that educates your audience on using specific products or services. This naturally fits into affiliate marketing by linking to relevant products.
- **Niche-Specific Partnerships:** Join affiliate programs that align with your content niche, ensuring the products are relevant and valuable to your audience.

Sponsorships

- **Direct Brand Sponsorships:** As your platform grows, you can secure sponsorship deals directly from brands interested in reaching your audience.
- **Content Series Sponsorships:** Develop a series of content on a particular topic and secure a sponsor for the entire series, offering consistent exposure over a set period.
- **Event and Webinar Sponsorships:** Expand your content to include live events or webinars, providing another avenue for sponsorship revenue.

Digital Products

- **EBooks and Courses:** Package your expertise into digital products such as eBooks, online courses, or downloadable guides, directly monetizing your knowledge.
- **Subscription Services:** Offer premium content through memberships or subscription services, such as exclusive videos, behind-the-scenes content, or personalized consulting.
- **Merchandise:** Leverage your brand by selling merchandise such as branded apparel, accessories, or digital art created using AI tools like Midjourney.

Niche Strategy and Consistency

The digital marketplace is vast, and standing out requires a focused niche strategy. Niche selection involves identifying a specific target audience and developing content that addresses their particular interests and pain points.

Finding Your Niche

- **Research Trends:** Use AI tools to analyze market trends, identify popular topics, and assess the competition. Tools like Google Trends and social media analytics can provide valuable insights.
- **Audience Feedback:** Engage with your audience through comments, polls, or surveys to determine what content they find most valuable.

49

- **Passion and Expertise:** Focus on areas where you have both interest and expertise. Authenticity resonates with audiences and builds trust over time.

Maintaining Consistency

Consistency in content creation is critical for sustained growth. Here are some strategies to stay consistent:

- **Content Calendar:** Develop a content calendar using Notion AI or other scheduling tools to plan topics, production timelines, and publishing dates.
- **Batch Production:** Create multiple pieces of content in one session. For example, script several video ideas at once using ChatGPT, or design multiple graphics using Canva.
- **Set Realistic Goals:** Define what "consistent" means for you. Whether it's one video per week or two blog posts per month, setting a manageable schedule is key to avoiding burnout.
- **Iterate Based on Feedback:** Regularly review analytics and audience feedback to refine your content strategy. A data-driven approach helps ensure that your content remains relevant and engaging.

Example Workflow: From Idea to Upload

Let's walk through a detailed example workflow that demonstrates how to harness AI at every stage of content creation—from ideation to publishing—using a hypothetical project.

Assume you're creating a YouTube video that will also be repurposed into short TikTok clips and a supportive blog post.

Step 1: Ideation and Planning

Brainstorming with ChatGPT:

- You start by asking ChatGPT: "What are some engaging topics for a YouTube video about the latest trends in eco-friendly technology?"
- ChatGPT suggests several ideas such as innovations in renewable energy gadgets, smart home devices for sustainability, and startups focusing on green technology.

Visual Inspiration with Midjourney:

- Next, you use Midjourney to generate a series of images that capture the essence of eco-friendly technology.
- These images help define the aesthetic and mood for the video, such as nature-inspired color palettes and minimalist design elements.

Content Calendar Setup:

- Using Notion AI, you organize your ideas into a content calendar.
- You schedule specific deadlines for scripting, filming, and editing to ensure a consistent workflow.

Step 2: Scripting and Storyboarding

Drafting the Script:

- With a clear topic and aesthetic in mind, you prompt ChatGPT for a first draft of the script. For example:
- *"Write a 800-word script for a YouTube video on eco-friendly technology trends, including statistics, expert quotes, and a call to action to follow for more sustainable living tips."*
- The output gives you a structured script that you can refine further.

Storyboarding:

- Alongside the script, create a simple storyboard using Canva, outlining key visual elements for each section of the video.
- This ensures that your visuals align with the narrative and helps you plan shots or transitions.

Step 3: Filming and Voiceover

Recording the Content:

- With the script in hand, record your video. To save time, you may record a single take and let the editing process refine the final output.

Voiceover Editing with Descript:

- Import your audio into Descript, which automatically tran-

scribes the spoken words.
- Edit the transcript to remove filler words and awkward pauses, then use the overdub feature to replace any sentences if needed.

Step 4: Video Editing and Production

Editing with Pictory and Runway ML:

- Upload the raw footage into Pictory to trim long segments and extract the best moments. Pictory helps generate short highlight clips suitable for repurposing on TikTok.
- For more advanced editing—such as background removal or color correction—use Runway ML to fine-tune the visuals.

Adding Captions and Graphics:

- Integrate captions automatically generated by Descript to enhance accessibility.
- Use Canva to design overlay graphics or call-out text that reinforces key points in the video.

Step 5: Publishing and Repurposing

Optimizing for SEO and Scheduling:

- For YouTube, write a compelling title, description, and keyword-rich tags. Use an SEO tool to refine your metadata.
- Schedule your video for release at a time when your analytics indicate peak viewership.

Repurposing for TikTok:

- Extract the best 60-second segments from your YouTube video using Pictory and upload them to TikTok.
- Tailor the captions and hashtags specifically for the TikTok audience.

Supporting Blog Post:

- Repurpose the script into a blog post, adding images, screenshots, or additional commentary where necessary.
- Optimize the blog post with relevant keywords and links to your YouTube channel and TikTok profile, creating a cross-promotion ecosystem.

Step 6: Post-Publishing Analysis and Iteration

Monitoring Performance:

- Use analytics tools to track how well your video, TikTok clips, and blog posts perform in terms of engagement and reach.
- Pay attention to key metrics like watch time, click-through rates, and audience retention.

Gathering Feedback:

- Encourage viewers to leave comments and provide feedback. Use this input to refine future content.

Iterating Based on Data:

- Adjust your content strategy based on audience responses and performance metrics. This might involve changing the video length, updating the style of graphics, or experimenting with different posting times.

Strategic Considerations for AI-Powered Content Creation

Niche Focus and Audience Building

When working within your chosen niche, consistency and authenticity are paramount. Here's how to maintain a successful niche strategy:

- **Define Your Audience:** Understand the demographics, interests, and pain points of your target audience. Use AI tools and social media analytics to gain insights.
- **Tailor Your Messaging:** Ensure that every piece of content—from video scripts to blog posts—speaks directly to your niche. Use language and examples that resonate with your audience.
- **Establish Authority:** Regularly share valuable insights, tutorials, and expert opinions. Over time, your consistency will establish you as a trusted source in your niche.

Consistent Content Production

Building an audience relies on a steady stream of content. Consistency is achieved through careful planning:

- **Set a Publishing Schedule:** Determine a realistic cadence for content publication. Whether it's weekly videos or bi-weekly blog posts, stick to your schedule.
- **Leverage Automation:** Use AI-powered scheduling tools to automate the publication of your content across multiple platforms. This frees up more time for creative processes.
- **Monitor Trends:** Use AI to track emerging trends in your niche. Adjust your content plan to incorporate new ideas without straying from your core focus.
- **Quality Control:** While speed is beneficial, quality should never be compromised. Use editing tools and feedback loops to ensure every piece of content meets your standards.

Monetization Revisited: Turning Creativity into Income

As you implement the above workflow, remember that multiple monetization avenues can help sustain and grow your content creation efforts. Here's a recap of the primary paths:

- **Ad Revenue:** Rely on ad placements and platform-specific monetization programs (like YouTube Partner Program) to generate income as your viewership grows.
- **Affiliate Links:** Integrate relevant affiliate offers into your

content. For instance, if you're reviewing tech gadgets, include affiliate links to purchase those products.

· **Sponsorships:** As your reputation builds, reach out to or attract sponsors. Develop packages for sponsored content series or integrations within your videos.

· **Digital Products:** Leverage your expertise to create digital assets like eBooks, courses, or exclusive content accessible through memberships.

Understanding which paths work best for your niche and audience will depend on continuously testing, analyzing, and iterating your approach.

Final Thoughts

AI-powered content creation has reshaped the way creators conceptualize, produce, and monetize their work. The blend of advanced ideation, scripting, editing, and publishing tools empowers creators to focus on what truly matters—delivering value and engaging stories to their audience.

By adopting top AI tools such as Pictory for video editing, Descript for efficient audio/video refinement, Runway ML for creative visual effects, ChatGPT for scripting and ideation, and Midjourney for visual inspiration, you can establish a robust workflow that minimizes manual effort and maximizes output. Coupled with a well-thought-out monetization strategy that includes ad revenue, affiliate marketing, sponsorships, and digital product sales, you're well-positioned to build a sustainable content business.

A key takeaway is the importance of a niche strategy and consistency. Identifying a clear target audience, tailoring your messaging, and producing high-quality content on a regular basis builds trust and authority. Over time, this consistent quality output not only attracts more viewers but also opens multiple revenue streams, ensuring your creative efforts yield long-term financial rewards.

The detailed example workflow—from brainstorming with ChatGPT and Midjourney to editing with Descript and publishing on YouTube and TikTok—illustrates that every step of the process can be powered by AI. When these elements come together seamlessly, you transform complex production pipelines into streamlined systems that allow you to focus on creativity and strategic growth.

In conclusion, the future of content creation is dynamic and integrative. Embracing AI doesn't just automate tasks; it catalyzes your creative process, enabling you to explore, experiment, and evolve continuously. Whether you're just launching your first blog or refining a multi-platform digital strategy, AI-powered content creation tools open up a world of possibilities. Every idea you nurture, every script you refine, and every video you edit brings you one step closer to building a thriving, monetized content empire.

Harness the power of AI, experiment with new formats, and refine your workflow consistently. With time and persistence, the fusion of technology and creativity will help you carve out a unique space in the crowded digital landscape, turning passion into profit and ideas into influence.

Welcome to the era where your creative vision meets intelligent automation—a collaboration that redefines the art and business of content creation. The journey from ideation to upload is now faster, smarter, and richer than ever before. Enjoy the exploration and watch as your creative efforts translate into tangible success in the ever-evolving digital gold rush.

4

Chapter 4: AI-Generated Books & Audiobooks

In today's digital era, the power of artificial intelligence is not only limited to sparking creative ideas or boosting productivity—it has also opened up entirely new avenues for creating and monetizing content. One of the most exciting opportunities is the ability to generate books and audiobooks almost entirely with AI. This chapter will explore how you can harness AI tools to write, format, publish, and market both eBooks and audiobooks, creating a passive income stream that scales over time. We'll cover tools like ChatGPT, Sudowrite, and Claude for writing, discuss the intricacies of formatting and selling on Amazon KDP, explain how to create audiobooks using ElevenLabs and Play.ht, and dive into strategies for marketing your digital content through Instagram and email sequences. Finally, we will conclude with a comprehensive case study of launching a passive income book series.

Writing and Publishing with AI Tools

The advent of advanced AI writing tools has revolutionized how content is generated, making it possible to create entire books with minimal human intervention. These tools are designed to assist you with idea generation, drafting, editing, and refining your work so that the final product is both engaging and market-ready.

AI Writing Tools: ChatGPT, Sudowrite, and Claude

ChatGPT

ChatGPT is one of the foremost tools available for content creation. It is capable of generating text based on prompts, making it a powerful assistant in the early stages of writing. You can use ChatGPT to brainstorm ideas, outline chapters, or even produce the first draft of your book. Its ability to mimic natural language and adjust tone according to the input makes it incredibly versatile. For instance, if you're writing a business guide or a narrative-driven novel, you can simply instruct ChatGPT to "Draft an engaging introduction for a book on AI innovation," and it will provide a coherent passage that you can then refine and build upon.

Sudowrite

Sudowrite is another AI tool tailored for creative writing. It offers functionalities like expanding existing text, suggesting plot twists, and even rewriting passages for better flow and impact. Sudowrite is particularly useful when you're struggling with writer's block or need fresh inspiration. It helps transform rough drafts into polished narratives. Its intuitive interface and creative prompts mean that writers can explore multiple ideas quickly, selecting the most compelling direction for their work.

Claude

Claude, a competitive AI writing assistant, offers similar capabilities to ChatGPT and Sudowrite but with its own unique style and algorithms. It can provide alternative perspectives on topics, generate concise summaries, and even assist with research by suggesting relevant sources and references. Claude is particularly effective when used alongside other AI tools, offering a second layer of scrutiny and creative input which is invaluable for fine-tuning your manuscript.

Collaborative AI Writing Process

The process of writing a book using these AI tools can be broken down into several phases:

- **Brainstorming and Outlining:** Start with a clear topic or theme. Use ChatGPT to generate a list of potential chapter headings and ideas. Create a mind map or outline using these ideas, ensuring that your book follows a logical structure.
- **Drafting:** Use ChatGPT or Sudowrite to produce the initial draft of your chapters. This can be done chapter by chapter, with AI generating multiple iterations until you find a version that resonates.
- **Editing and Refinement:** Once the draft is complete, run it

through editing tools. Utilize Claude to suggest improvements and ensure that the tone, clarity, and pacing of the book meet professional standards.

· **Final Proofreading:** Use traditional tools like Grammarly for final checks on grammar, spelling, and punctuation to ensure that the text is polished.

By leveraging these tools, you transform the laborious process of book-writing into a dynamic, iterative cycle of creativity and refinement.

Formatting and Selling on Amazon KDP

After your manuscript is refined and finalized, the next step is formatting your content for publication. Amazon Kindle Direct Publishing (KDP) is one of the most popular platforms for indie authors, offering unparalleled reach and ease of access to a global audience.

Formatting Your eBook

Formatting your book properly is crucial for a good reader experience. AI tools and templates simplify this task by ensuring that your text is cleanly formatted for e-readers and mobile devices. Here are the key steps:

· **Manuscript Preparation:** Begin by exporting your final draft from your AI writing tool. Use tools like Microsoft Word or Scrivener, which offer built-in templates designed specifically for KDP. These templates help ensure that your margins, fonts, and chapter headings are consistent throughout.

- **Conversion to eBook Formats:** The most common formats for eBooks are MOBI and EPUB. Tools like Calibre or Kindle Create can help convert your manuscript seamlessly. Kindle Create, for example, is designed specifically for Amazon KDP and integrates with KDP's guidelines, allowing you to preview your book on different devices.
- **Cover Design:** An eye-catching cover is vital for attracting readers. Use AI-powered design tools like Canva, which offer templates and design elements that are perfectly sized for Amazon KDP. The cover should not only be visually appealing but should also reflect the theme and tone of your book.

Publishing on Amazon KDP

Publishing on Amazon KDP is relatively straightforward, but success requires attention to detail:

- **Account Setup:** Create an Amazon KDP account and fill out the necessary tax and payment information.
- **Book Details:** Enter your book's title, subtitle, description, and keywords. These elements are critical for searchability and attracting potential readers.
- **Upload Files:** Upload your formatted manuscript and cover image. Kindle Create allows you to do a final preview, so ensure that every chapter and element appears as intended.
- **Pricing and Royalties:** Set your book's price and choose your royalty option (typically 35% or 70%). Consider re-

searching similar titles in your niche to select a competitive price point.

- **Launch:** Once everything is ready, publish your book. After publication, your eBook is available on Amazon's global marketplace, where it can reach millions of readers.

With Amazon KDP, the barriers to entry are lower than ever, making it a perfect platform for AI-generated content.

Creating Audiobooks with AI Tools

While eBooks remain a popular format, the rise of audiobooks is undeniable. Audiobooks cater to an increasingly mobile audience and can significantly expand your market reach. AI technologies have also advanced in the realm of audiobook production, making the process more accessible and cost-effective.

Utilizing ElevenLabs and Play.ht

ElevenLabs

ElevenLabs specializes in creating natural-sounding AI voices. This tool can transform your written content into engaging audio narration, which is crucial for delivering an audiobook that captivates listeners. With a range of voice options and emotional tone settings, ElevenLabs allows you to choose a voice that best fits your book's theme. The tool also offers customizable pacing and intonation to ensure the narration feels organic and professional.

Play.ht

Play.ht is another powerful text-to-speech tool that offers high-quality voice synthesis. It supports multiple languages and accents, making it ideal for reaching a diverse audience. Beyond simple conversion, Play.ht provides editing functionalities that allow you to adjust pronunciation and emphasis. This flexibility ensures that the final audio version of your book is both accurate and pleasant to listen to.

Creating the Audiobook

The process of converting your eBook into an audiobook involves several key steps:

- **Script Preparation:** Adapt your manuscript into a script suitable for audio consumption. This might involve simplifying complex passages or adding auditory cues to guide the listener.
- **Voice Selection:** Choose a voice that best represents your book. Experiment with different options in ElevenLabs and Play.ht to find the right match for your narrative style.
- **Audio Editing:** Once the narration is generated, use audio editing software to refine the audio. Remove any errors, awkward pauses, or background noise. This step is crucial in ensuring that the final product is smooth and professional.
- **Finalization and Distribution:** After editing, export the audio files into a suitable format (MP3 or AAC are common).

These files can then be uploaded to platforms like Amazon Audible via ACX (Audiobook Creation Exchange), ensuring that your audiobook reaches a wide audience alongside your eBook.

By using AI to produce audiobooks, you can cater to those who prefer listening over reading—a market that continues to grow.

Marketing with AI Tools

Creating a book or audiobook is only part of the equation; effective marketing is what drives sales and converts your content into a sustainable income stream. AI-powered marketing tools can help you reach your target audience efficiently and cost-effectively.

Instagram Content and Social Media Marketing

Social media is a cornerstone of modern marketing strategies, and Instagram remains one of the most visually engaging platforms. AI tools can help you produce consistent, targeted content:

- **Content Creation:** Use AI tools like Canva (integrated with AI design suggestions) to create engaging visuals, infographics, and short video clips that highlight the key themes of your book or audiobook.
- **Caption Writing:** ChatGPT can help generate compelling captions that drive engagement and link back to your book

landing page or Amazon listing.

- **Analytics:** Use AI-powered analytics tools to monitor your engagement, track which types of posts perform best, and optimize your posting schedule. This ensures that your content is reaching the right audience at the right time.
- **Hashtag Strategy:** AI tools can analyze trending hashtags within your niche, helping you adopt a hashtag strategy that increases visibility and attracts new followers.

Email Sequences and Automation

Email marketing is another potent channel for promoting your digital content. Building an email sequence not only helps nurture a relationship with your audience but also drives repeat sales and builds a loyal fan base.

- **Lead Magnets:** Offer a free chapter or exclusive content preview in exchange for email sign-ups. AI tools can help generate compelling lead magnet content that persuades visitors to subscribe.
- **Sequence Creation:** Use email marketing platforms like Mailchimp or ConvertKit, many of which now integrate AI for subject line optimization and email sequencing. AI can analyze engagement data and suggest improvements to boost open and click-through rates.
- **Personalization:** Leverage AI to personalize emails based on subscriber behavior. For example, segment your audience based on which topics or genres they are interested in, and tailor your email content accordingly.
- **Automation:** Set up automated follow-up sequences that nurture your leads until they are ready to purchase your

book or audiobook. Automation ensures that you stay in touch without manual intervention, saving you time and effort.

Cross-Promotion and Content Integration

Integrating your marketing efforts across multiple channels creates a cohesive ecosystem that drives traffic and sales. For instance:

- **Social Media to Email:** Encourage your Instagram followers to join your email list with enticing calls-to-action.
- **Blog Content:** Write blog posts that provide deeper insights into the topics discussed in your book, linking back to both the eBook and audiobook versions.
- **Podcast Interviews:** Use AI to generate outreach emails and pitches to podcast hosts in your niche, expanding your reach even further.

Case Study: Launching a Passive Income Book Series

To illustrate how all these elements come together in a real-world scenario, let's consider the journey of Samantha, an indie author who leveraged AI to launch a successful passive income book series.

The Genesis

Samantha was a marketing consultant with a passion for sharing her knowledge on digital marketing, social media trends, and business growth. Realizing that her expertise could be repackaged into digital products, she decided to write a series of books titled "Digital Marketing Mastery." However, Samantha wasn't a natural-born writer, and her busy schedule made traditional writing methods almost impossible. That's when she turned to AI.

Writing the First Book

Using ChatGPT and Sudowrite:

Samantha started by using ChatGPT to brainstorm content ideas and generate an outline for her first book. She provided detailed prompts such as "Outline a book on digital marketing trends for small businesses in 2024." The generated outline served as a perfect foundation, and she then used Sudowrite to expand on sections that needed more creative flair. Within weeks, she had a full draft that covered everything from social media strategies to SEO, complete with actionable tips and case studies.

Editing and Refinement with Claude:

Once the draft was complete, Samantha used Claude to review and refine the manuscript. Claude provided suggestions for clearer transitions between chapters and improved the overall tone, ensuring that the final product was both engaging and professional.

Formatting and Publishing on Amazon KDP

Formatting the eBook:

After polishing her manuscript, Samantha formatted the book using Kindle Create. The tool's built-in templates helped her ensure that the layout was consistent and reader-friendly. She then converted the file to the required formats (MOBI and EPUB) and designed an eye-catching cover using Canva. With every element in place, she uploaded her book to Amazon KDP, complete with a compelling book description and carefully selected keywords.

Setting the Pricing and Launch:

Samantha chose a competitive pricing strategy based on market research and opted for the 70% royalty option. She strategically set the launch date to coincide with a social media campaign she planned to execute across her channels.

Creating the Audiobook

Text-to-Speech Conversion:

Recognizing the growing popularity of audiobooks, Samantha decided to convert her eBook into an audiobook. Using ElevenLabs, she selected a natural-sounding narrator voice that matched the tone of her content. She imported her manuscript into the tool, which generated a clean audio narration with the right pacing and intonation.

Refinement with Play.ht:

To ensure the audio quality was impeccable, Samantha used Play.ht to fine-tune pronunciation and emphasize key parts of the narration. After a few rounds of editing and listening tests, she finalized the audiobook, preparing it for distribution via ACX (Audiobook Creation Exchange) and directly linking it with her Amazon listing.

Marketing the Book Series

Building the Social Media Presence:

Samantha set up an Instagram account dedicated to digital marketing tips, leveraging AI-powered content creation tools to produce daily posts, reels, and stories. With the help of ChatGPT, she crafted engaging captions that connected her social media content with her book series.

Email Sequence and Lead Magnet:

She created a lead magnet—a free downloadable guide on "Top 10 Digital Marketing Hacks"—and used AI tools integrated into her email marketing platform to develop an automated sequence. This sequence nurtured her audience over several weeks, guiding subscribers from initial interest to the final purchase of her book.

Cross-Promotion and Consistency:

To maximize her reach, Samantha used AI to repurpose content across platforms. Blog posts, YouTube videos, and even podcast interviews were all aligned with the themes in her book series. Her consistent messaging and high-quality content helped build trust with her audience, driving sustained sales and positive reviews.

The Outcome

Within six months, Samantha's passive income book series was not only generating steady monthly royalties from Amazon KDP and Audible, but it was also helping her build a loyal community of followers on social media and through her email list. The integration of AI tools saved her countless hours of work while maintaining a high standard of quality across all her digital products. This strategic use of AI not only established Samantha as an authority in digital marketing but also provided her with a scalable, passive income stream that continues to grow.

Integrating Your Workflow for Success

The journey from crafting an idea to launching and monetizing a fully-fledged book series or audiobook involves multiple steps, each of which can be streamlined using AI:

- **Idea Generation and Outlining:** Use ChatGPT and Midjourney to generate creative concepts and visual inspirations that form the backbone of your content.

- **Writing and Editing:** Leverage ChatGPT, Sudowrite, and Claude to draft and refine your manuscript. AI tools ensure the content is both high-quality and engaging.
- **Formatting and Publication:** Utilize Kindle Create and related software to format your eBook according to industry standards. Publish seamlessly on Amazon KDP and prepare marketing materials accordingly.
- **Audiobook Production:** Transform your written work into a compelling audiobook using ElevenLabs and Play.ht. Edit and refine until the audio quality matches your brand's standards.
- **Marketing and Promotion:** Create a multi-platform marketing strategy. Leverage Instagram content, email sequences, and cross-promotion tactics powered by AI to ensure that your work reaches the right audience.
- **Analytics and Iteration:** Finally, use analytics tools to track the performance of your books and audiobooks. AI-driven insights will help you refine your strategies over time, ensuring continued growth and improved engagement with your audience.

Final Thoughts

The integration of AI into the world of book and audiobook creation represents a groundbreaking opportunity. It allows you to turn ideas into published works with unprecedented speed and efficiency. Whether you are an experienced author or a newcomer to the realm of digital publishing, AI tools can amplify your creativity, streamline your workflow, and ultimately help you build a scalable, passive income stream.

By combining powerful writing assistants like ChatGPT, Sudowrite, and Claude with robust formatting, publishing, and marketing strategies on platforms such as Amazon KDP, Eleven-Labs, and Play.ht, you are setting up an ecosystem that works 24/7 to promote and sell your work. As demonstrated in Samantha's case study, the secret to success lies in a well-integrated workflow where creativity meets automation, resulting in high-quality content that resonates with a global audience.

Embrace this new frontier of AI-generated books and audiobooks. Let technology handle the heavy lifting while you focus on your unique ideas and creative vision. With patience, persistence, and the right tools, the opportunity to build a steady stream of passive income is not only within reach—it's waiting for you to harness its full potential.

Welcome to the future of digital publishing, where every word and every sound can be crafted with AI, opening doors to markets you never thought possible. Your journey from idea to passive income success is ready to begin—step forward and let artificial intelligence be your guide.

5

Chapter 5: E-Commerce + AI Automation

In the digital age, e-commerce has become one of the most accessible and scalable business models. Today, artificial intelligence is transforming every aspect of online retail, from product research and trend spotting to customer service and marketing. In this chapter, we will explore how to harness AI automation to build and grow an e-commerce business with minimal input. We'll cover everything from identifying profitable products using AI to automating the creation of product descriptions, ad copy, and visuals. You'll also learn how AI chatbots can revolutionize customer service and how to scale your operations efficiently. By integrating AI into your e-commerce strategy, you can streamline processes, reduce costs, and focus on scaling your business to new heights.

Product Research and Trend Spotting Using AI

Successful e-commerce begins with finding the right product niche. With a constantly evolving market landscape, staying on top of trends is crucial for long-term success. AI-powered tools have revolutionized product research by providing real-time data and insights that help identify emerging trends and untapped market opportunities.

Leveraging Big Data for Market Insights

AI excels at processing massive datasets, analyzing consumer behavior, and predicting future trends. Traditional product research methods, which involved manual market surveys and trend analysis, are time-consuming and often outdated by the time the findings are implemented. With AI, however, you can:

- **Analyze Consumer Behavior:** AI tools can track millions of customer interactions across social media, search engines, and e-commerce platforms. This data helps you understand what products are trending, what features consumers value, and how purchasing behavior is evolving.
- **Identify Seasonal Trends:** Using historical data and pattern recognition, AI can predict seasonal fluctuations and highlight the best times to launch or promote products.
- **Spot Market Gaps:** AI platforms can identify niches that are underserved by analyzing keyword trends, competitor activity, and customer feedback. This can lead to discovering products that meet specific consumer needs yet to be fully addressed by the market.

Tools for Product Research

Several AI tools are specifically designed for trend spotting in e-commerce. These tools provide actionable insights that streamline your product research process:

- **Google Trends and Social Listening Tools:** By analyzing search trends and social media mentions, these tools highlight rising interests and potential product opportunities. They can also pinpoint geographic areas where certain products are more popular.
- **E-commerce Analytics Platforms:** Platforms like Helium 10 and Jungle Scout use AI to provide detailed insights on product demand, competition, and profitability—essential for platforms like Amazon and Etsy.
- **AI-Powered Surveys:** Tools that integrate AI with customer surveys can provide predictive insights on product viability, ensuring that you invest in products with a promising market trajectory.

Integrating these tools into your research process means that you can quickly identify winning products without the guesswork typically involved in product selection.

AI Tools for Dropshipping, Print-on-Demand, and Etsy Stores

After identifying a profitable niche, the next step is to set up your online store. AI-driven platforms simplify various e-commerce models, including dropshipping, print-on-demand, and even niche marketplaces like Etsy.

Dropshipping and AI

Dropshipping is an attractive business model because it eliminates the need to hold inventory. When combined with AI, dropshipping becomes even more efficient:

- **Inventory and Supplier Management:** AI can monitor supplier inventories in real time and predict when products will run low, ensuring that your store always offers the best options to customers.
- **Order Fulfillment Optimization:** AI algorithms can automatically select the best suppliers based on price, shipping speed, and customer location, optimizing order fulfillment processes.
- **Automated Competitive Analysis:** Dropshipping platforms enhanced with AI can continuously track competitor prices and trends, enabling you to adjust your pricing strategies dynamically.

Print-on-Demand and AI

Print-on-demand allows you to sell customized products, such as apparel, accessories, and home decor, without dealing with inventory issues. AI tools can enhance this model by:

- **Design Generation:** AI-powered design tools like Adobe Sensei or Canva's AI features can help create unique product designs based on current trends and customer preferences.
- **Personalization Options:** AI can analyze customer data to suggest personalized design modifications, increasing the likelihood of conversion.
- **Production Efficiency:** Integrating AI with production partners can streamline the printing and shipping process, reducing turnaround times and costs.

Optimizing an Etsy Store with AI

Etsy is a popular marketplace for handmade, vintage, and unique items. AI can give sellers an edge by:

- **Search Optimization:** AI-powered SEO tools help optimize product titles, tags, and descriptions to ensure your listings appear in relevant searches.
- **Trend Forecasting:** AI can analyze buyer behavior on Etsy to predict which types of products or designs will be most popular, allowing you to plan your inventory in advance.
- **Customer Engagement:** Chatbots and automated messaging systems can respond to customer inquiries promptly, enhancing customer satisfaction and increasing the likelihood of repeat business.

Creating Product Descriptions, Ad Copy, and Visuals Automatically

Effective product listings require compelling descriptions, persuasive ad copy, and attractive visuals. AI can generate these components with minimal input, ensuring consistency and quality across your store.

Automating Product Descriptions

Writing unique and engaging product descriptions can be time-consuming, especially when you have a large catalog. AI tools such as ChatGPT, Jasper, or Copy.ai can help:

- **Tailored Descriptions:** By inputting basic product details, you can generate a detailed description that highlights key features, benefits, and uses. The AI can also incorporate SEO keywords naturally.
- **Scalability:** Once you establish a template, the AI can produce hundreds of descriptions quickly, freeing up your time to focus on other aspects of your business.
- **A/B Testing:** Use AI to create multiple versions of product descriptions and test which format drives more conversions.

Generating Ad Copy Automatically

Ad copy is critical for driving traffic to your online store. AI tools can generate persuasive copy for various platforms, including Google Ads, Facebook, and Instagram:

- **Dynamic Copy Creation:** Provide details about your product and target audience, and let the AI create variants of ad copy. This copy can be tested in real-time campaigns to find the best performing versions.
- **Personalization:** Advanced AI tools can adjust the tone and style of ad copy based on the platform or target demographic, ensuring that your message resonates with different audience segments.
- **Cost Efficiency:** Automated ad copy generation reduces the need for ongoing copywriting resources and enables quick pivots when market conditions change.

Creating Visuals with AI

Visual content is a driving force in e-commerce. High-quality images, videos, and graphics not only attract attention but also build trust with potential customers:

- **AI-Powered Image Editing:** Tools like Canva, Adobe Sensei, and Fotor use machine learning to enhance images, create branded templates, and generate engaging visuals automatically.
- **Video Content:** AI tools like Animoto and Magisto can create product videos by automatically compiling images, video clips, and music based on the product description.

- **Consistency Across Channels:** AI ensures that all visuals adhere to a consistent style and color scheme, crucial for building brand recognition across your website, social media, and ad campaigns.

By automating these creative processes, you can maintain a professional look and feel for your e-commerce store while saving significant time and resources.

Running Customer Service with AI Chatbots

Excellent customer service is the cornerstone of a successful e-commerce business. AI-powered chatbots are revolutionizing how businesses handle customer inquiries, support, and post-purchase follow-up.

The Role of AI in Customer Service

Customer service chatbots leverage natural language processing (NLP) and machine learning to provide instant and accurate responses to customer queries. The benefits of using AI chatbots include:

- **24/7 Availability:** Chatbots can assist customers at any time of day, ensuring that inquiries are answered promptly, regardless of time zones.
- **Cost Savings:** By automating routine interactions, AI chatbots reduce the need for a large customer service team, allowing you to allocate resources elsewhere.

- **Consistent Quality:** Chatbots provide standardized responses, reducing the likelihood of errors or miscommunication while maintaining a professional tone.
- **Scalability:** As your business grows, chatbots can handle increased traffic without a proportional increase in support staff, ensuring that customer satisfaction remains high.

Implementing AI Chatbots

Several platforms offer robust AI chatbot solutions that can be integrated into your e-commerce website:

- **Zendesk Answer Bot and Intercom:** These tools integrate seamlessly with your website and use AI to handle frequently asked questions, order tracking, and basic troubleshooting.
- **Custom Chatbot Solutions:** Platforms like Dialogflow by Google allow you to build a chatbot tailored to your specific business needs, complete with natural language understanding and personalized responses.
- **Social Media Integration:** Many AI chatbot solutions can also be integrated with social media platforms such as Facebook Messenger, providing consistent support across multiple channels.

Effective integration of chatbots can improve customer retention, reduce response times, and enhance the overall shopping experience—key factors in driving repeat business and positive reviews.

Scaling Your E-Commerce Business with Minimal Input

One of the primary advantages of using AI in e-commerce is the ability to scale operations with minimal additional input. The automation and efficiency afforded by AI tools mean that you can expand your business without a dramatic increase in operational overhead.

Automating Routine Tasks

AI enables you to automate various processes critical to scaling an e-commerce business:

- **Inventory Management:** With AI-powered systems, you can track stock levels, reorder products automatically, and predict when seasonal trends will affect demand, ensuring that you never miss a sale due to stock-outs.
- **Order Processing:** Automation tools can streamline order processing—from confirming payments and sending invoices to updating shipping details—reducing manual errors and speeding up the fulfillment cycle.
- **Analytics and Reporting:** AI tools can continuously monitor key performance indicators (KPIs) and generate real-time reports. These insights allow you to make data-driven decisions and rapidly adjust your strategy based on performance metrics.
- **Email Marketing Automation:** Set up automated email campaigns for abandoned carts, post-purchase follow-

ups, and promotional offers. This keeps your customers engaged without requiring constant manual oversight.

Scaling Marketing Efforts

Expanding your customer base is essential for scaling any e-commerce business. AI-driven marketing solutions enable you to reach more customers with less effort:

- **Ad Campaign Optimization:** AI tools can manage and optimize your ad campaigns in real time, adjusting bids and targeting to maximize return on investment (ROI).
- **Personalized Marketing:** Use customer data and AI to segment your audience and deliver personalized marketing messages that drive higher conversion rates.
- **Influencer and Affiliate Marketing:** AI platforms can identify potential influencers and affiliates in your niche, streamlining the process of establishing partnerships that expand your reach.

Enhancing Operational Efficiency

As your business grows, integrating AI into your operations ensures that scaling doesn't compromise quality or customer satisfaction:

- **Task Automation:** Routine tasks such as data entry, customer follow-ups, and inventory audits can be automated using AI-powered software, freeing you to focus on strategic growth initiatives.
- **Integration of Systems:** Use AI to connect different parts

of your business ecosystem—from your e-commerce platform and customer service to marketing and analytics—creating a cohesive, self-optimizing system.

- **Continuous Learning:** Leverage AI-driven feedback and machine learning algorithms to continually improve your systems. This proactive approach to operational efficiency can reduce costs and improve overall performance.

By automating both customer-facing and backend tasks, AI allows you to manage increasing volumes of orders, customer inquiries, and marketing campaigns without a proportional increase in workload.

Case Study: Scaling an AI-Driven E-Commerce Store

To bring these concepts to life, let's examine the journey of Marcus, an entrepreneur who built a successful AI-driven e-commerce business that scales with minimal manual intervention.

The Beginning

Marcus started his venture with a passion for sustainable home decor. After identifying a market gap in eco-friendly, stylish home accessories, he decided to launch an online store focused on these products. Rather than investing heavily in traditional inventory, Marcus opted for a dropshipping model, relying on AI tools to manage most of his operations.

Product Research and Trend Identification

Using AI-powered tools, Marcus was able to:

- **Analyze Consumer Preferences:** By studying social media trends and e-commerce data, he quickly identified which eco-friendly products were trending.
- **Select the Right Products:** AI analytics helped him pick a curated list of items that were not only popular but also offered good profit margins. These insights allowed him to make data-driven decisions, minimizing risk.

Building the Store with AI

Marcus integrated several AI solutions to streamline his operations:

- **Automated Product Listings:** He used AI to generate compelling product descriptions and optimized images, ensuring that his listings were both attractive and SEO-friendly.
- **Customer Service Automation:** Implementing an AI chatbot on his site enabled instant responses to customer queries. This led to increased customer satisfaction and reduced the need for a full-time support team.
- **Marketing Automation:** Marcus set up automated email marketing campaigns and leveraged AI-driven social media tools to schedule and optimize his posts. This consistent effort drove steady traffic to his store.

Scaling Up

Within six months, Marcus's store experienced rapid growth:

- **Increased Orders:** As his product listings and marketing campaigns took off, the volume of orders increased significantly, all handled by his automated systems.
- **Improved Efficiency:** AI systems managed inventory, order processing, and customer service seamlessly, allowing Marcus to focus on strategic expansion and new product research.
- **Cost Savings:** By automating routine tasks, Marcus reduced overhead costs substantially, which in turn increased his profit margins.

The Outcome

Today, Marcus's AI-driven e-commerce store is a thriving business with minimal daily input from him. His automated systems ensure that everything—from customer inquiries to order fulfillment—is handled efficiently. The use of AI has not only saved him time and money but also enabled him to scale his business rapidly. This success story is a testament to how embracing AI in e-commerce can lead to sustainable, scalable growth.

Integrating AI Automation into Your E-Commerce Strategy

As you embark on your e-commerce journey, consider the following steps to successfully integrate AI automation into your strategy:

- **Start with the Right Tools:** Begin by researching and selecting AI platforms for product research, customer service, and marketing. Experiment with different solutions to find those that best match your business needs.
- **Design a Scalable Workflow:** Map out your entire e-commerce process—from product selection and listing to order fulfillment and customer support—and identify areas where AI can streamline operations.
- **Automate Key Tasks:** Implement AI-driven automation for routine tasks. Focus on areas that have the highest impact on efficiency, such as product listings, customer queries, and marketing campaigns.
- **Monitor and Optimize:** Use AI analytics tools to track performance in real time. Regularly review data to identify bottlenecks, fine-tune workflows, and continuously improve your systems.
- **Focus on Customer Experience:** Even as you automate, never lose sight of the customer experience. Ensure that your AI-driven interactions remain personal and responsive.
- **Plan for Continuous Growth:** As your business scales, integrate additional AI solutions to handle increasing volumes. A phased approach will help you maintain quality while expanding your operations.

Final Thoughts

AI automation is revolutionizing e-commerce, transforming it into a highly efficient, scalable business model. By leveraging AI for product research, marketing, customer service, and operational efficiency, you can build an e-commerce store that grows with minimal manual input. The integration of AI tools not only reduces overhead costs but also enhances the quality of your product listings, advertising, and customer interactions.

Whether you choose dropshipping, print-on-demand, or a niche marketplace like Etsy, AI offers the flexibility and power to simplify every aspect of your business. As demonstrated by Marcus's success story, automation paves the way for increased productivity and profitability, allowing you to concentrate on strategic decision-making rather than day-to-day tasks.

The journey to scaling an e-commerce business with AI is dynamic and continuously evolving. Embrace the tools available, experiment with different strategies, and leverage data-driven insights to stay ahead of the competition. In this new era of digital commerce, AI isn't just a tool—it's a strategic partner that can propel your business to new heights.

By combining meticulous product research, robust AI-powered automation, and a relentless focus on customer experience, you can build an e-commerce business that not only survives but thrives. The future of online retail is smart, automated, and incredibly scalable. Step into this future with confidence, and let AI transform your vision into a sustainable, profitable reality.

Welcome to the era of e-commerce automation, where every facet of your business is optimized for efficiency, creativity, and growth. Harness this technology, and watch as your online store evolves into a powerhouse of innovation and profitability with minimal intervention.

6

Chapter 6: Investing & Trading with AI

In today's data-rich and fast-paced financial markets, artificial intelligence is rapidly transforming how investments are made and trades are executed. From stock analysis to cryptocurrency trading, AI-powered tools and algorithms have emerged as game changers, providing deeper insights, automating decision-making, and enabling faster, more accurate trades. However, with great potential comes notable challenges and risks. In this chapter, we will provide an in-depth exploration of the application of AI in investing and trading. We will cover the latest AI-powered stock analysis tools and trading bots, discuss the risks and limitations of algorithmic trading, explore the opportunities offered by crypto and AI integration, and provide guidance on building or using AI trading assistants. Finally, we will address the critical issues of compliance and the necessary caution flags every investor and trader should be aware of.

AI-Powered Stock Analysis Tools and Bots

Revolutionizing Financial Analysis

Traditional financial analysis often involves sifting through historical data, reading through earnings reports, and manually analyzing market trends. With the explosion of data sources and market complexity, these methods can be labor-intensive and limited by human cognitive capacity. AI-powered tools have revolutionized this process by processing vast amounts of data in real time, recognizing patterns, and even forecasting market trends with a speed and precision that far exceeds human capability.

Modern AI stock analysis tools use algorithms to:

- **Aggregate Data:** They collect and integrate information from diverse sources such as financial statements, market news, social media sentiment, and macroeconomic indicators.
- **Identify Patterns:** By applying machine learning techniques, these tools can detect non-linear patterns and hidden correlations that might be missed in traditional analysis.
- **Generate Predictions:** AI models provide predictive analytics based on historical trends, which help in forecasting future price movements and estimating risk.
- **Automate Decision-Making:** Some advanced systems can automatically execute trades based on preset criteria—these are the trading bots that operate in milliseconds.

94

Key AI Tools in Stock Analysis

Several specialized platforms have emerged that leverage AI to aid investors:

- **QuantConnect and Alpaca:** These platforms integrate quantitative trading with machine learning, enabling users to develop custom algorithms, backtest strategies, and deploy live trading bots.
- **Tickeron:** An AI-driven tool that provides technical analysis signals, predictive pattern recognition, and trade ideas based on real-time market data.
- **Trade Ideas:** Known for its AI-powered "Holly" system, which uses machine learning to scan millions of potential trades, devise strategies, and alert traders to high-probability opportunities.
- **Kavout:** Uses AI and machine learning to produce stock ratings and predictions, helping investors make better-informed decisions by analyzing patterns across multiple data sets.

These tools are designed not only for institutional investors but also for retail investors who wish to gain a competitive edge. They allow users to set custom parameters, run simulations, and optimize trading strategies, thereby transforming the decision-making process into a more data-driven exercise.

Automated Trading Bots

Automated trading bots are software programs that use AI algorithms to execute trades automatically based on predefined rules and strategies. Unlike manual trading, bots operate 24/7, taking advantage of market opportunities as soon as they arise. Their capabilities include:

- **Speed:** Bots can execute thousands of trades per second, capturing small inefficiencies in the market that can lead to significant cumulative profits.
- **Emotion-Free Decision Making:** By removing human emotion from the equation, bots help avoid common pit-falls such as panic selling or overexposure during bullish runs.
- **Strategy Implementation:** They can seamlessly implement complex trading strategies including momentum trading, arbitrage, and market making.
- **Risk Management:** Automated systems can incorporate risk management protocols such as stop losses, limits, and diversification strategies, ensuring that the potential downside is minimized even while capturing gains.

Through continuous improvement driven by machine learning, automated trading bots are becoming more sophisticated, adapting to changing market conditions and continuously refining their algorithms over time.

Risks and Limitations of Algorithmic Trading

Despite its many advantages, algorithmic trading is not without its risks and limitations. As markets become increasingly automated, understanding these challenges becomes essential for both professional and retail investors.

Market Volatility and Unexpected Events

AI models depend heavily on historical data to predict future trends. However, unprecedented events—such as geopolitical tensions, sudden regulatory changes, or global pandemics—can significantly disrupt market patterns. These "black swan" events are notoriously hard to predict and may render historical models ineffective. During high volatility, AI-driven models might generate false positives or misinterpret rapid changes, leading to substantial losses.

Overfitting and Model Limitations

One of the critical pitfalls in AI and algorithmic trading is the risk of overfitting. Overfitting occurs when an algorithm is too closely tailored to historical data, capturing noise rather than underlying trends. An overfitted model may perform exceptionally well during backtesting but fail to generalize in real-time market conditions. Common manifestations include:

- **Reduced Flexibility:** Overfitted models may be less responsive to new market data, leading to outdated strategies.
- **Poor Generalization:** While past performance might appear robust, these models often falter in unanticipated

market conditions.

- **Data Snooping Bias:** The more parameters and variables an algorithm considers, the higher the likelihood of identifying a coincidental pattern rather than a true predictive signal.

Technical and Operational Risks

Algorithmic trading relies on complex software and stable infrastructure. Technical glitches, such as server downtimes, connectivity issues, or software bugs, can cause significant disruptions. Additionally, unintended algorithmic errors may trigger unintended market orders or exacerbate losses during adverse conditions.

Regulatory and Ethical Considerations

Regulators are increasingly scrutinizing algorithmic trading due to its potential to influence market stability. Issues such as market manipulation, flash crashes, and systemic risks have prompted increased oversight. Traders and developers must ensure that their algorithms comply with regulatory standards to avoid fines, sanctions, or reputational damage. Ethical concerns also arise when AI-driven decisions lead to unfair practices, such as insider trading or market manipulation tactics that could harm smaller investors.

Crypto + AI Opportunities

The integration of AI into cryptocurrency trading represents one of the most exciting frontiers in modern finance. Cryptocurrencies, due to their high volatility and decentralized nature, provide fertile ground for applying AI technologies.

The Appeal of Cryptocurrencies

Crypto markets operate 24/7, are influenced by global factors, and often react rapidly to news and events. This round-the-clock trading environment makes manual trading challenging, creating a demand for automated systems that can analyze data in real time and act instantly. Additionally, the relatively less regulated nature of crypto markets compared to traditional financial markets allows for greater flexibility in algorithmic trading.

AI in Crypto Trading

AI and machine learning can process vast amounts of on-chain data, social media sentiment, and trading volumes to identify trends and potential arbitrage opportunities in crypto markets. Some of the specific applications include:

- **Sentiment Analysis:** AI tools can analyze public sentiment on platforms like Twitter, Reddit, and Telegram to gauge the market mood. These insights can be critical in predicting short-term price movements.
- **Price Prediction Models:** By analyzing historical price patterns, volatility, and trading volume, AI models can

forecast potential price movements for cryptocurrencies such as Bitcoin, Ethereum, and altcoins.

- **Arbitrage Bots:** AI-driven bots can identify and exploit price differences between various cryptocurrency exchanges. Given the fragmented nature of crypto markets, these opportunities often arise and are quickly capitalized upon.
- **Risk Management:** In highly volatile crypto markets, AI can automatically adjust strategies to minimize potential losses through dynamic risk management techniques, such as adaptive stop-loss orders and position sizing based on volatility analysis.

Challenges in Crypto Trading

While AI offers significant opportunities in crypto trading, it also faces challenges:

- **Market Manipulation:** Cryptocurrencies can be more susceptible to manipulation by large holders ("whales"), and AI models need to be robust enough to handle such distortions.
- **Data Quality:** Crypto markets suffer from issues related to data reliability and standardization across different exchanges. This can make training AI models more complex.
- **Regulatory Uncertainty:** The regulatory landscape for cryptocurrencies is still evolving. Changes in regulations can dramatically affect market dynamics and the effectiveness of AI-driven strategies.
- **Security Risks:** Given the digital nature of cryptocurrencies, security is paramount. AI systems must be safeguarded

against hacking attempts and other forms of cybercrime.

Building or Using AI Trading Assistants

For those interested in harnessing the power of AI for trading, there are two primary approaches: building your own AI trading assistant or using existing platforms.

Building Your Own AI Trading Assistant

Building an AI trading system from scratch offers maximum customization but also requires advanced technical skills, including knowledge of machine learning, quantitative finance, and software development. Here are the key steps:

- **Define Objectives and Strategies:** Determine the type of trading strategy you want to implement (e.g., momentum trading, mean reversion, arbitrage) and define clear performance metrics.
- **Data Collection and Processing:** Gather historical and real-time data from multiple sources, including financial markets, news feeds, and social media. Use preprocessing techniques to clean and standardize the data.
- **Model Development:** Build machine learning models using frameworks such as TensorFlow or PyTorch. Experiment with various algorithms (e.g., neural networks, decision trees) and perform backtesting to evaluate the model's performance.
- **Integration and Automation:** Once the model is trained and

validated, integrate it with a trading platform using APIs. Automate trade execution based on the model's signals while incorporating risk management protocols.

· **Monitoring and Improvement:** Continuously monitor the performance of your trading assistant. Use feedback loops to retrain and fine-tune your model as market conditions evolve.

Building your own system gives you complete control but also demands significant time, resources, and expertise.

Using Commercial AI Trading Platforms

For many traders, using ready-made AI trading platforms is a more practical solution. These platforms offer plug-and-play solutions that require minimal technical know-how:

· **Subscription-Based Services:** Many providers offer AI trading algorithms as a subscription service. This allows you to benefit from sophisticated models without having to build them from scratch.

· **White-Label Solutions:** Some platforms offer white-label solutions that you can customize and brand as your own while they manage the technical aspects.

· **Integration with Brokerages:** Platforms like QuantConnect, Alpaca, and Trade Ideas offer seamless integration with popular brokerages, enabling you to implement AI-driven strategies with minimal effort.

These solutions often come with comprehensive support, documentation, and regular updates, making them an attractive option for retail investors and smaller institutions.

Compliance and Caution Flags

While AI offers extraordinary advantages in trading, a high degree of vigilance is required to avoid pitfalls and remain compliant with regulatory standards.

Regulatory Compliance

Regulatory bodies worldwide are increasingly scrutinizing the use of AI and algorithmic trading. To comply, investors and developers need to:

- **Adhere to Reporting Requirements:** Ensure that all trading activities are properly reported and documented. Many jurisdictions require detailed records of algorithmic trading activities.
- **Implement Risk Management Protocols:** Regulators often mandate robust risk management frameworks. This includes setting and monitoring stop losses, limits on trade sizes, and ensuring systems can handle extreme market conditions.
- **Transparency and Auditing:** Maintain transparency regarding your AI models' decision-making processes. Regular audits and updates to your trading algorithms can help demonstrate compliance with regulatory standards.
- **Data Privacy:** Be cognizant of data privacy regulations such as GDPR or CCPA. If your AI trading system uses personal

data, ensure that it is handled in compliance with applicable laws.

Caution Flags

AI-driven trading is not foolproof. Here are some caution flags that every trader should heed:

- **Over-Reliance on Automation:** Relying solely on automated trading without human oversight can lead to unexpected losses, particularly during periods of market instability.
- **Model Uncertainty:** Recognize that AI models are based on historical data which may not always predict future anomalies. Maintain a level of skepticism regarding model outputs.
- **Black-Box Algorithms:** Some AI systems operate as "black boxes" where the decision-making process is not transparent. This can be risky if you cannot fully understand or explain why certain trades are executed.
- **System Failures:** Be prepared for technical issues. Regular system backups, failover protocols, and human intervention plans should be in place to manage potential breakdowns.
- **Market Manipulation and Ethical Concerns:** Stay alert to the ethical implications of algorithmic trading. Ensure that your strategies do not inadvertently contribute to market manipulation or systemic risk.

By balancing the power of AI with a clear understanding of its limitations and maintaining a robust compliance framework, you can mitigate the risks involved in algorithmic trading.

Integrating AI into a Comprehensive Trading Strategy

To benefit fully from AI in trading, it is essential to integrate these technologies into an overarching strategy that combines human judgment with machine efficiency. Here are key steps in developing such an integrated approach:

Define Clear Objectives

Before deploying any AI system, clearly define your financial goals, risk tolerance, and time horizon. Whether you are aiming for steady income, high-growth potential, or a balanced portfolio, your objectives will guide the selection of strategies and models.

Combine AI with Human Oversight

AI should function as an aid rather than a replacement for human decision-making. Regularly review AI-generated strategies and adjust them as necessary. Establish clear checkpoints for human intervention to ensure that the AI's output aligns with your broader investment philosophy.

Continuous Learning and Adaptation

Markets are dynamic, and AI models need to evolve to remain effective. Implement a feedback loop where market performance is continuously monitored, and the models are updated and retrained based on new data and changing conditions. This proactive approach allows you to adapt to market cycles and emerging trends.

Diversify Your Approach

Relying on a single AI model or trading strategy can be risky. Diversify across multiple approaches—such as short-term trading, long-term investments, and arbitrage opportunities—to mitigate overall risk. Using multiple AI systems in conjunction allows you to balance out weaknesses in any one model.

Emphasize Risk Management

Integrate robust risk management protocols into your trading strategy. Establish clear guidelines for position sizing, stop-loss orders, and portfolio rebalancing. Employ AI tools specifically designed for risk analysis to help maintain a balanced and diversified portfolio.

Real-World Application: A Hypothetical Case Study

To illustrate the integration of AI into an investment strategy, consider the case of Elena, a retail investor aiming to build a diversified portfolio using both traditional stocks and cryptocurrencies.

Setting the Stage

Elena began by outlining clear objectives: she sought moderate long-term growth with manageable risk. Using AI tools, she performed an extensive analysis of the stock market and crypto space, evaluating trends, volatility, and market sentiment.

Developing the Trading Strategy

- **Stock Analysis:** Elena used QuantConnect and Trade Ideas to analyze historical data and identify undervalued stocks with strong fundamentals. AI algorithms helped her pinpoint market inefficiencies and forecast potential price movements.
- **Crypto Opportunities:** In the volatile crypto market, Elena implemented sentiment analysis tools and arbitrage bots that continuously monitored price discrepancies across exchanges. This allowed her to take advantage of brief arbitrage opportunities while balancing her exposure in leading cryptocurrencies.
- **Risk Management:** Integrating AI risk analysis tools, Elena established dynamic stop-loss orders and diversified her investments across multiple sectors and asset classes. This approach was fine-tuned using backtesting, ensuring that

her risk parameters were in line with her overall investment strategy.

Execution and Continuous Monitoring

Elena's AI trading assistant was set to operate within predefined parameters, executing trades automatically while flagging any significant deviations for her review. Through continuous monitoring via an AI dashboard, she was able to see real-time performance metrics, market trends, and potential adjustments recommended by the system.

Outcome

Over a period of 12 months, Elena's diversified portfolio showed consistent growth despite periods of market turbulence. By leveraging AI to guide her decisions and automate trades, she minimized emotional decision-making and achieved improved risk-adjusted returns. The success of her approach underscored the importance of combining advanced technology with disciplined oversight.

Final Thoughts

The landscape of investing and trading is undergoing a profound transformation as artificial intelligence becomes an integral part of financial decision-making. AI-powered stock analysis tools and automated trading bots offer unprecedented speed, insight, and precision. Yet, as with any powerful technology, risks and limitations—such as overfitting, technical failures, and market anomalies—must be managed with care.

In the realm of cryptocurrencies, AI opens up further opportunities, from sentiment analysis to arbitrage, though it also brings unique challenges such as data quality and regulatory uncertainty. Whether you build your own AI trading system or choose a commercial platform, incorporating human judgment and robust risk management is essential for long-term success.

Compliance remains a critical pillar of responsible AI trading. Ensuring adherence to regulatory standards, implementing thorough risk management protocols, and being vigilant about ethical considerations are non-negotiable aspects of leveraging AI in the financial markets.

In conclusion, merging AI with investing and trading offers a potent combination that can unlock significant gains and streamline the decision-making process. However, this path requires continuous learning, prudent risk management, and a commitment to ethical practices. By thoughtfully integrating AI into your trading strategy—balancing technological prowess with human oversight—you position yourself to navigate the complexities of modern financial markets with confidence and clarity.

Welcome to the future of investing and trading, where every trade is powered by data, every decision is informed by advanced algorithms, and every risk is managed through intelligent automation. Embrace the possibilities, remain cautious, and continually adapt your strategies to ensure that AI serves as your most valuable tool in building a robust and dynamic investment portfolio.

7

Chapter 7: Building and Selling AI Tools or SaaS

The AI revolution is not limited to content creation, trading, or marketing—it also presents a tremendous opportunity for entrepreneurs to build and sell AI-powered tools or software-as-a-service (SaaS) products. Whether you're a technical expert or someone with minimal coding experience, the advent of no-code and low-code platforms has democratized the process of developing AI applications. In this chapter, we'll explore how to harness these technologies to create tools that solve real problems, package powerful models like GPT or other large language models (LLMs), and monetize your innovations through subscriptions, one-time sales, or lead generation.

We'll cover the following key areas:

- No-Code and Low-Code Tools to Build Simple AI Apps
- Finding Problems Worth Solving
- Packaging GPT or LLM Wrappers
- Monetization Strategies: Subscriptions, One-Time Sales,

Lead Generation
· Examples of Successful Small AI Apps

Each section of this chapter is designed to walk you through the process of conceiving, building, and commercializing your own AI-powered tool or SaaS product.

No-Code and Low-Code Tools to Build Simple AI Apps

The New Frontier of Software Development

Traditionally, building a software application required extensive coding knowledge and a deep understanding of technology stacks. The rapid development in no-code and low-code platforms has changed that landscape dramatically. These platforms enable you to develop fully functional AI applications with little or no prior programming experience. The benefits include faster development cycles, reduced costs, and the ability to iterate quickly on your ideas.

Popular No-Code/Low-Code Platforms

· **Bubble:** A comprehensive no-code platform that allows you to build interactive, multi-user apps for desktop and mobile browsers. Bubble supports API integrations and can connect to AI services easily, making it a popular choice for SaaS startups.
· **Zapier and Integromat (now Make):** These platforms

automate workflows between different applications. They can help you integrate AI models (like those from OpenAI) into your business process without writing extensive code.

- **Microsoft PowerApps:** Part of the broader Microsoft Power Platform, PowerApps allows you to create custom apps that work on both web and mobile with a minimal coding footprint. It can integrate with various data sources and AI modules.
- **Webflow:** While primarily a website builder, Webflow's advanced design and CMS capabilities paired with API integrations allow you to create AI-powered web experiences.
- **Airtable:** Combining the simplicity of a spreadsheet with the power of a database, Airtable can be connected to various AI tools through its API and automation features, making it a flexible tool for prototyping SaaS ideas.

How These Tools Accelerate AI App Development

No-code and low-code platforms lower the barrier to entry by abstracting much of the complexity involved in app development. With drag-and-drop interfaces, pre-built templates, and robust integration capabilities, you can:

- Quickly prototype ideas and test market fit.
- Implement iterative development without extensive coding cycles.
- Focus on design, user experience, and functionality rather than the underlying infrastructure.

These platforms are particularly powerful when combined with AI APIs, allowing you to harness the cutting-edge capabilities of large language models (LLMs) and other AI services with minimal technical overhead.

Finding Problems Worth Solving

The Importance of Problem Identification

The foundation of any successful SaaS or AI tool is its ability to solve a real problem. Before you start building, it's vital to identify issues or pain points that your potential customers are experiencing. The best ideas often come from areas where technology can offer significant improvements—either by automating tedious tasks, enhancing decision-making, or providing new ways of engaging with data.

Methods for Identifying Opportunities

- **Market Research:** Start by analyzing market trends and consumer behavior. Use AI-powered analytics tools (like Google Trends, SEMrush, or industry-specific tools) to discover what topics or problems are frequently discussed in your target market.
- **Customer Feedback:** Engage with potential customers via surveys, social media groups, forums, or platforms like Reddit. Listen to their challenges and frustrations. What repetitive tasks do they wish were automated? What information do they struggle to access quickly?
- **Competitive Analysis:** Study existing tools and apps in your domain. Identify gaps in their functionality, usability

issues, or areas where customer reviews indicate dissatis-faction. This could reveal opportunities for you to offer a better alternative.

- **Personal Experience:** Often, the problems you face in your day-to-day work can spark innovative ideas. Reflect on the challenges you've encountered—if you've ever thought, "There must be a better way to do this," that might be a sign of an unmet need.

Validating the Problem

Once you've pinpointed a potential problem, validation is crucial:

- **Minimum Viable Product (MVP):** Create a basic version of your app or tool using no-code platforms to test with early adopters. Gather feedback and assess whether the problem is significant enough to warrant a full-scale solution.
- **Pilot Programs:** Engage a small group of target users to test your concept. Monitor their engagement, solicit feedback, and adjust based on their responses.
- **Data Analysis:** Use analytics to determine whether your tool solves the problem effectively. Look for improvements in efficiency, cost savings, or user satisfaction compared to traditional methods.

By validating that the problem is both significant and solvable, you reduce the risk of investing time and resources into a solution that doesn't have a market.

Packaging GPT or LLM Wrappers

What Is a Wrapper?

A wrapper is essentially an application layer that provides a user-friendly interface to complex underlying technology. In the context of GPT or other large language models, a wrapper simplifies interactions with the AI, allowing users to submit queries, receive outputs, and integrate results into their workflows without needing to understand the intricacies of the API or model internals.

Why Package AI Models?

- **Accessibility:** Packaging a language model into an easy-to-use application democratizes access to advanced AI, making it useful even for those without technical backgrounds.
- **Customization:** You can tailor the wrapper to address specific use cases, such as customer service automation, content generation, or data analysis.
- **Monetization:** A well-designed wrapper can be sold as a stand-alone product or offered as part of a broader SaaS solution, creating new revenue streams.

Steps to Packaging a GPT or LLM Wrapper

- **Define the Use Case:** Identify specific problems your wrapper will solve. For instance, a wrapper that helps businesses generate ad copy or a tool that assists with real-time content moderation.

- **Design the User Interface:** Focus on usability and simplicity. Ensure that users can easily input data, receive results, and understand how to customize outputs.
- **Integrate the AI API:** Use platforms such as OpenAI's API to connect your wrapper to the underlying GPT model. Low-code platforms and developer tools often provide simple ways to integrate these APIs.
- **Test and Refine:** Conduct thorough testing with potential users, refining the interface and adding features based on feedback.
- **Document the Tool:** Provide clear documentation and tutorials to help users get started. This can include video guides, step-by-step instructions, and FAQs.

Enhancing the Wrapper with Additional Features

- **Analytics and Reporting:** Integrate analytics so users can track how their interactions with the tool translate into tangible outcomes.
- **Customization Options:** Allow users to tweak parameters such as tone, style, or focus areas to better suit their needs.
- **Integration with Other Tools:** Enable seamless integration with popular platforms like CRM systems, content management systems, or project management tools. This enhances the value proposition by embedding the AI directly into existing workflows.

Monetization Strategies: Subscriptions, One-Time Sales, Lead Generation

Once your AI tool or SaaS product is built, the next step is to choose a monetization strategy that aligns with your business model and target market. There are several approaches you can take, either individually or in combination.

Subscription-Based Revenue

- **Recurring Income:** Subscription models provide predictable, recurring income. Users pay on a monthly or yearly basis, ensuring a steady revenue stream.
- **Tiered Pricing:** Offer multiple tiers based on usage levels. For instance, a basic plan might include limited queries or features, while a premium plan offers unlimited access, advanced customization, and priority support.
- **Free Trials:** Attract users with a free trial period. This allows potential subscribers to experience the value of your tool before committing to a subscription.

One-Time Sales

- **Licensing:** Sell a one-time license for your software, often with limited updates or support.
- **Perpetual Licensing:** Charge a higher price for a perpetual license that grants lifetime access. This model is less common in SaaS but can work well for specialized tools.
- **Add-Ons and Upgrades:** Even with one-time sales, you can offer paid add-ons or premium features to enhance the base product, creating additional revenue opportunities.

Lead Generation and Freemium Models

- **Freemium Approach:** Offer a basic version of your tool for free, then monetize through premium features or services. This model can attract a large user base and drive upselling.
- **Lead Generation:** Use the tool as a means to collect leads for higher-value services. For example, if your tool is aimed at content creators, it could capture contact information to later market consulting services, workshops, or advanced training courses.
- **Partnerships and Affiliate Marketing:** Integrate your tool within larger ecosystems or partner with influencers who can drive traffic and generate revenue through affiliate links.

Advertising Integration

If your tool garners significant user engagement, you could integrate advertising as an additional revenue stream. This might include in-app advertisements or sponsored content, provided it does not detract from user experience.

Examples of Successful Small AI Apps

The market is already witnessing a surge in small AI apps that have successfully tapped into niche markets. Here are a few examples that illustrate the potential of this approach:

Content Generation Tools

Copy.ai and Jasper: These tools leverage GPT-based models to help users generate marketing copy, blog content, and social media posts. They offer subscription-based models with tiered pricing options. Their success is built on the ability to simplify the content creation process and produce quality outputs in a fraction of the time it would take a human.

Customer Service Chatbots

Chatfuel and ManyChat: While not exclusively AI-generated, these platforms enable businesses to create sophisticated chatbots that improve customer engagement and support. They have successfully monetized through subscription models by offering continuous support and updates, demonstrating how automated tools can drive substantial value for businesses.

Niche Data Analysis Tools

Crimson Hexagon (now part of Brandwatch): This tool uses AI to analyze social media and online content, providing businesses with insights into customer sentiment and market trends. By packaging complex data into understandable dashboards, it has carved out a niche in the analytics market.

Personalization Engines

Persado: Persado uses AI to generate personalized messaging for marketing campaigns. By understanding customer behavior and language preferences, the platform optimizes communication strategies, which has led to successful adoption by large brands. This demonstrates how AI can be used to drive tangible business outcomes, even in sophisticated areas like customer engagement.

AI-Powered SaaS for Specific Industries

LegalRobot: This AI-driven tool offers legal document analysis and compliance checks. By packaging complex legal language into digestible insights, it addresses a clear pain point in the legal industry, providing a model for how niche SaaS products can succeed.

Integrating Your Product into a Business Strategy

Beyond building the tool itself, successful entrepreneurs integrate their AI product into a broader business strategy. Here are key considerations for long-term success:

Customer Focus

Keep the user at the center of your development process. Regularly solicit feedback and iterate on your product. A tool that genuinely helps users solve a problem will naturally attract loyal customers and positive word-of-mouth, which is critical for growth.

Marketing and Community Building

Develop a marketing strategy that leverages social media, content marketing, and SEO. Many successful AI tools have built communities around them—forums, webinars, and social media groups where users can share tips and best practices. This not only improves retention but also provides valuable insights for future development.

Strategic Partnerships

Form alliances with other players in your industry. Whether it's integrating with complementary tools or forming partnerships with influencers and thought leaders, these collaborations can extend your reach and add credibility to your product.

Scaling and Automation

As your user base grows, automation becomes key. Use AI-driven analytics and customer relationship management (CRM) systems to monitor user behavior, manage support tickets, and optimize your marketing campaigns. The goal is to scale operations without diluting the quality or customer satisfaction.

A Hypothetical Success Story: From Idea to Market Domination

Consider the story of Daniel, a digital entrepreneur who iden-tified a gap in the market: many small businesses struggled to generate effective, on-brand social media content quickly. Daniel set out to build a no-code AI tool that packaged GPT-based content creation into an easy-to-use app.

Identifying the Problem

Through market research and customer interviews, Daniel discovered that small business owners often wasted time trying to create content that resonated with their audience. They wanted an affordable, efficient solution that could generate social media posts, email campaigns, and blog snippets.

Building the Solution

Daniel used a no-code platform to create a prototype of his tool. He integrated the OpenAI API and designed a simple interface that allowed users to input a few keywords and receive tailored content options. Using feedback from early testers, he refined the interface and added features such as tone adjustment and content templates.

Packaging and Monetizing

Realizing the broader potential of his tool, Daniel packaged it as a SaaS product with a freemium model. The basic version was free, with premium features available on a subscription basis.

He also offered one-time purchases for specialized templates. A well-thought-out affiliate program further boosted his user base as digital marketing influencers began promoting his product.

Launch and Growth

Daniel's product quickly gained traction. By leveraging social media marketing, content marketing (via blogs and webinars), and targeted email campaigns, he built a strong community of loyal users. The success of his tool is now reflected in robust subscription numbers and consistent revenue growth—a testament to how a small AI-powered SaaS product can transform a passion for problem-solving into a scalable business.

Final Thoughts

The landscape of AI tools and SaaS products is rich with opportunities for entrepreneurs willing to solve real problems through innovative technology. With no-code and low-code platforms lowering the barrier to entry, even those with limited technical skills can create impactful applications. By focusing on pain points, packaging powerful AI capabilities into user-friendly wrappers, and choosing the right monetization strategy, you can build a sustainable business that capitalizes on the global AI revolution.

Remember that the key to success lies in continuously iterating on your product based on user feedback, building a strong brand through effective marketing, and forming strategic partnerships that enhance your offering. Whether you opt for a subscription model, one-time sales, or a hybrid approach, the goal is to create a product that delivers clear, measurable value to its users.

As you develop your AI tool or SaaS product, consider the examples of successful small AI apps as both inspiration and proof of concept. Their success stories demonstrate that there is a significant market for niche, high-quality digital tools that harness AI's power.

In summary, building and selling AI tools or SaaS products is about combining creative problem-solving with the latest technology. With the right blend of technology, market insight, and business acumen, you can tap into the modern AI gold rush—transforming innovative ideas into sustainable, profitable ventures. Embrace this opportunity, and let your entrepreneurial journey in the world of AI begin.

8

Chapter 8: The AI Consultant Path

In the modern business landscape, artificial intelligence is no longer a futuristic technology—it's a powerful tool that companies of all sizes can leverage to boost efficiency, drive innovation, and gain a competitive edge. However, integrating AI into existing workflows is not always straightforward. This is where the role of an AI consultant becomes invaluable. In this chapter, we will explore the multifaceted role of the AI consultant: helping businesses adopt AI, auditing workflows, suggesting the best tools for their unique needs, training teams to embrace the technology, creating automation solutions using tools like Zapier and Make, pricing and pitching your services effectively, and using various tools to deliver client projects faster. By the end of this chapter, you'll have a comprehensive roadmap to build a successful career as an AI consultant.

Helping Businesses Adopt AI

The AI Opportunity for Businesses

Today's companies are inundated with data and complex work-flows that often require significant manual labor. The promise of AI lies in its ability to automate routine tasks, derive insights from large datasets, and drive innovation in decision-making processes. For many businesses, especially small to medium-sized enterprises (SMEs) and startups, the leap into AI can seem intimidating due to limited resources and expertise. This is where an AI consultant comes in—by acting as a bridge between cutting-edge technology and practical business applications.

As an AI consultant, your mission is to demystify the technology for businesses. You help them understand not only what AI is but how it can be specifically applied within their organization. This often starts with identifying pain points and inefficiencies in current workflows, then mapping out AI-driven solutions that can optimize operations, reduce costs, and improve overall competitiveness.

Identifying Business Needs and Opportunities

Every business is different, and the value of AI lies in its adaptability. To help companies adopt AI, you first need to perform a detailed assessment of their processes. This involves:

- **Evaluating Existing Workflows:** Assess how data flows through the organization and pinpoint processes that are redundant or time-consuming.

127

- **Understanding Strategic Goals:** Align AI opportunities with the company's broader strategic objectives. Whether it's increasing sales, enhancing customer service, or improving operational efficiency, your recommendations should support their mission.
- **Conducting Market Research:** Analyze industry trends and competitor strategies to identify emerging technologies that could be applied to the business.
- **Stakeholder Interviews:** Engage with key team members to understand their daily challenges and gather insights on areas where AI might streamline operations.

By conducting comprehensive audits, you can uncover "low-hanging fruit" where even simple AI applications can generate significant improvements, and then scale up to more complex implementations over time.

Auditing Workflows, Suggesting Tools, and Training Teams

Auditing Client Workflows

The cornerstone of effective AI consulting is a thorough audit of current business processes. This involves mapping out workflows, identifying bottlenecks, and determining where manual efforts could be replaced or augmented with automated solutions.

- **Workflow Analysis:** Begin by diagramming the client's

processes from start to finish. Tools like flowchart software (Lucidchart, Microsoft Visio) or simple whiteboarding techniques can help visualize these steps.

· **Data Collection:** Gather both quantitative and qualitative data. Look at productivity metrics, error rates, processing times, and employee feedback.

· **Process Mapping:** Create detailed maps that highlight where data is input, processed, and output. Identify redundancies, inefficiencies, or error-prone areas that could benefit from automation.

· **Technology Audit:** Review any current technological tools and software the client uses. Determine whether these tools are integrated properly or if there are gaps that more modern AI solutions could fill.

Recommending AI Tools and Solutions

Based on the workflow audit, you can then recommend specific AI tools and platforms tailored to the client's needs. This may include:

· **Predictive Analytics Tools:** For data-heavy operations where forecasting trends or customer behavior is key.

· **Natural Language Processing (NLP) Tools:** If the business handles significant volumes of unstructured text data, such as emails, support tickets, or social media content.

· **Robotic Process Automation (RPA):** Tools like UiPath or Automation Anywhere that can automate repetitive tasks.

· **Chatbots and Virtual Assistants:** For customer service or internal support, AI-powered chatbots can handle routine inquiries effectively.

When suggesting tools, consider ease of integration, scalability, and cost-effectiveness. Your goal is to provide solutions that deliver measurable improvements without causing disruption to daily operations.

Training Teams to Embrace AI

Once the right tools have been selected, the next step is to ensure that the team can use them effectively. This training can be a critical factor in the successful adoption of AI.

- **Customized Training Programs:** Develop training sessions tailored to the client's specific needs. This could include on-site workshops, online webinars, or one-on-one coaching sessions.
- **Creating User Guides and Tutorials:** Develop comprehensive documentation and video tutorials that explain how to use the new tools. This not only helps during the initial rollout but also serves as a valuable reference for the future.
- **Workshops and Ongoing Support:** Schedule follow-up sessions to address issues or questions that arise post-implementation. Encourage a culture of continuous learning where team members feel empowered to experiment and innovate.
- **Change Management:** Emphasize the benefits of AI, such as reduced repetitive tasks and enhanced decision-making capabilities, to counteract any resistance to change. Highlighting success stories and tangible improvements can foster a more positive attitude towards new technology.

Effective training is about more than just technical skills—it's about cultivating an AI-ready mindset across the organization.

Creating Simple Automation Solutions with Zapier, Make, and Similar Tools

The Power of Automation in Business

One of the most accessible ways to demonstrate immediate value through AI consulting is by implementing automation solutions. Tools like Zapier, Make (formerly Integromat), and similar platforms enable businesses to connect disparate systems and automate routine tasks with minimal coding. These solutions can streamline workflows, improve data accuracy, and free up valuable time for strategic activities.

Setting Up Automation Workflows

- **Identifying Automation Opportunities:** Start by identifying repetitive tasks that take up a significant portion of employee time. This could include data entry, email responses, lead tracking, or social media posting.
- **Mapping Out Automation Flows:** Use a visual tool to map out the steps of the process you want to automate. Define triggers, actions, and conditions that govern the workflow.
- **Integrating Tools:** Connect existing systems—such as CRMs, email marketing platforms, and social media accounts—with automation tools. For example, you can use Zapier to automatically add new leads from a website form into a CRM, send a welcome email via Mailchimp, and

update a central spreadsheet.

- **Testing and Refining:** Before full-scale rollout, conduct rigorous testing. Monitor the workflow closely, gather feedback, and make necessary adjustments to ensure that the automation delivers as expected.

Real-World Examples of Automation in Action

Consider a marketing agency that spends considerable time on routine tasks:

- **Lead Nurturing Automation:** When a potential client fills out a contact form, Zapier can trigger a sequence where the lead is immediately added to an email campaign, tagged based on interest, and followed up with personalized automated messages.
- **Social Media Scheduling:** Integration with tools like Buffer or Hootsuite can automatically schedule posts based on pre-defined content calendars. When a new blog post is published, an automation workflow can share the link on social media channels.
- **Data Synchronization:** Automate the process of syncing customer data between the website's CRM and the sales team's tools, ensuring that everyone has access to the most up-to-date information.

These automation solutions not only save time but also reduce the likelihood of human error—delivering consistent, reliable outcomes.

How to Price and Pitch Your Services

Pricing Models for AI Consulting

Pricing your consulting services correctly is crucial for both attracting clients and ensuring your business is profitable. Several pricing models are commonly used in consulting:

- **Hourly Rates:** Charge clients based on the amount of time spent on a project. This model is straightforward but can discourage efficiency.
- **Project-Based Fees:** Charge a flat rate for completing an entire project. This approach is attractive to clients who prefer knowing the total cost upfront and rewards you for efficiency.
- **Retainers:** Establish an ongoing relationship where clients pay a monthly fee for continuous support and consultation. This model provides predictable income and fosters long-term client relationships.
- **Value-Based Pricing:** Set your fees based on the value you're providing to the client rather than the time spent. If your AI solution is projected to save a company significant money or drive substantial revenue, you can price your services as a percentage of that value.

Crafting a Compelling Pitch

When pitching your services, focus on the tangible benefits your expertise will bring to the client:

- **Identify Pain Points:** Clearly articulate the inefficiencies or challenges the client is facing and how AI can address these issues.
- **Showcase ROI:** Use case studies and data to demonstrate the potential return on investment. Explain how automated workflows, enhanced decision-making, and improved operational efficiency can lead to measurable gains.
- **Tailor Your Message:** Personalize your pitch to the client's industry, size, and specific needs. Avoid generic presentations; instead, focus on how your solutions will solve their unique problems.
- **Highlight Your Experience:** Share success stories and testimonials from previous projects. If you have quantifiable success metrics (like a percentage increase in efficiency or revenue growth), make sure to highlight these.
- **Offer a Pilot Program:** For hesitant clients, propose a pilot program with a limited scope and clear, measurable outcomes. This reduces their risk and provides you with an opportunity to demonstrate your value.

Positioning Yourself in a Competitive Market

Differentiation is key. Many businesses are now looking to adopt AI, so how can you stand out from the crowd? Emphasize your holistic approach:

- **End-to-End Service:** Instead of just recommending tools, offer a comprehensive package that includes audits, recommendations, implementation, training, and ongoing support.
- **Customization:** Highlight your ability to create bespoke solutions tailored to each client's specific workflow and business model.
- **Proven Methodologies:** Demonstrate that your approach is backed by both industry best practices and a track record of successful implementations.

By carefully pricing your services and crafting a compelling pitch, you can effectively communicate your value proposition and secure new clients.

Tools to Create Client Deliverables Faster

Time is money, and in the world of consulting, quick turnaround and high-quality deliverables can set you apart. Leveraging AI and digital tools can accelerate the process of creating proposals, reports, and other client materials.

Document and Presentation Creation

- **Notion and Trello:** Use these tools to organize your work and track project progress. Notion is especially useful for creating rich, interactive documents that can serve as both internal documentation and client deliverables.
- **Google Workspace/Microsoft Office:** Standard office tools

like Google Docs and PowerPoint remain essential. Enhance these with AI features (such as Google's Smart Compose) to speed up writing and formatting.

- **Canva:** For designing presentations, reports, and infographics, Canva offers a robust suite of templates and design tools. Its AI-assisted features help maintain consistent branding and professional aesthetics across deliverables.

Automated Reporting and Analytics

- **Dashboard Tools:** Platforms like Tableau, Power BI, or even Google Data Studio help you generate interactive, real-time dashboards for clients. These dashboards can consolidate data from multiple sources and provide insights that inform decision-making.
- **Report Automation:** Use scripting and automation (via tools like Zapier or custom Python scripts) to automatically populate regular reports with the latest data. This eliminates the need for manual data entry and ensures that reports are always up-to-date.

Communication and Collaboration

- **Slack or Microsoft Teams:** These messaging platforms, enhanced with AI bots, can streamline communication with clients. For instance, automated reminders and integrations with project management tools keep clients informed about project status.
- **Client Portals:** Consider setting up a secure client portal where clients can access deliverables, progress reports, and communicate with your team. This transparency builds

trust and improves client satisfaction.

By utilizing these tools, you can deliver high-quality client projects faster, freeing up your time to take on more work and enhance your overall productivity.

A Hypothetical Success Story: The AI Consultant Journey

Imagine a consultant named Alex who specializes in helping mid-sized manufacturing companies adopt AI to streamline their operations. Alex begins by auditing the company's workflow, identifying that manual data entry, inventory tracking, and customer service are major pain points. Alex then recommends a suite of AI tools, including RPA for inventory management, chatbots for customer service, and AI-powered analytics for forecasting demand.

After demonstrating the potential ROI through a pilot project— where the company saw a 20% reduction in operational costs and a 15% increase in productivity—Alex successfully pitches a long-term retainer model. Over the next six months, Alex trains the company's staff on the new systems, implements automation with tools like Zapier and Make to streamline data flows, and continuously refines the processes based on real-time analytics provided via dashboards.

As the success stories start accumulating, Alex's reputation grows, and more companies in similar industries seek out his expertise. To further improve his efficiency, Alex adopts productivity tools like Notion for project management, Trello for workflow tracking, and Canva for creating visually compelling reports. With each new project, Alex refines his pricing strategy—moving from hourly rates to value-based pricing as his impact on clients' bottom lines becomes evident.

By the end of the first year, Alex's consulting practice not only drives tangible improvements for clients but also evolves into a scalable business model. His success is built on a deep understanding of business needs, an effective use of no-code tools for implementation, and a strong focus on ongoing support and training. This comprehensive, results-driven approach cements his status as a trusted AI consultant.

Final Thoughts

The role of an AI consultant is both challenging and rewarding. It requires a blend of technical expertise, business acumen, and exceptional communication skills. By helping businesses adopt AI, auditing workflows, suggesting tailored tools, training teams, and creating simple yet effective automation solutions, you create immense value. Your role is not only to implement technology but also to foster a culture of innovation and continuous improvement within organizations.

Key takeaways for building a successful AI consulting practice include:

- **Understanding Client Needs:** Start with an in-depth audit of current workflows, identify inefficiencies, and map out where AI can make a tangible difference.
- **Leveraging No-Code Tools:** Utilize platforms like Zapier, Make, and various low-code solutions to quickly prototype and implement automation without heavy technical overhead.
- **Training and Empowerment:** Provide thorough training and ongoing support to ensure that clients can fully leverage the new tools, fostering long-term transformation.
- **Effective Pricing and Pitching:** Develop pricing models that reflect the value you provide and craft customized pitches that address the specific pain points of your clients.
- **Efficiency in Deliverables:** Use modern tools for project management, reporting, and design to create client deliverables quickly and professionally.

The future of AI consulting is bright, with increasing demand as more businesses strive to harness the power of intelligent automation. By staying ahead of technological trends, continuously refining your approach, and maintaining a laser focus on client outcomes, you can carve out a niche in this rapidly expanding field. Embrace the role of a trusted advisor and partner, helping companies navigate the complexities of AI adoption while positioning yourself as an indispensable resource for innovation and growth.

Welcome to the AI consultant path—a journey where you enable transformation, drive efficiency, and unlock the immense potential that AI offers to modern businesses. Step forward with confidence, armed with the knowledge, tools, and strategies outlined in this chapter, and embark on a career that not only fuels your entrepreneurial spirit but also reshapes the way businesses operate in the digital age.

9

Chapter 9: Affiliate Marketing for AI Tools

In the rapidly evolving world of AI technology, opportunities abound for those willing to become experts, critics, and marketers of these powerful tools. Affiliate marketing for AI platforms not only allows you to generate revenue by sharing insights about the latest applications, but it also positions you as a trusted voice in the AI space. In this chapter, we will delve into the strategies for reviewing, demoing, and promoting AI platforms. We'll explore content strategies across TikTok, YouTube, blogs, and newsletters, and show you how to scale your efforts with email automation and mass content production. We will also discuss how to become an authority in a specific AI niche and present a playbook for building a passive income stream based on affiliate marketing for AI tools.

Reviewing and Demoing AI Platforms

One of the most effective ways to engage with your audience in the affiliate marketing space is by creating high-quality reviews and demos of AI platforms. This process involves not only testing and evaluating the tools yourself but also delivering the findings in a clear, insightful, and engaging manner.

To start, choose a selection of AI tools that have high relevance and potential in the market. These might include AI writing assistants like ChatGPT and Jasper, design tools such as Canva with integrated AI features, data analysis platforms, and automation tools like Zapier or Make. As you review these platforms, pay attention to several key aspects:

- **Ease of Use:** Assess how user-friendly the interface is. How quickly can a new user begin to see value? This is particularly important for affiliate marketing since your audience will often consist of individuals who may not be tech experts.
- **Features and Functionality:** Identify the standout features of each platform. Can the tool generate creative ideas, automate tasks efficiently, or produce high-quality outputs? Be sure to demonstrate these features in your demos.
- **Performance and Reliability:** Evaluate the performance of the tool, including the speed of processing and the quality of the output. Reliability is a critical selling point for any software.
- **Pricing and Value:** Understand the pricing structure— whether it's subscription-based, usage-based, or comes with a one-time fee—and weigh it against the value the

tool delivers. Consider offering comparisons with similar products to provide context.

· **Customer Support and Community:** Examine what kind of support the platform offers. Are there comprehensive help articles, active user communities, or accessible customer service channels? Good support can be a deciding factor for many potential users.

Creating comprehensive reviews and demo videos not only educates your audience but also builds trust. It shows that you have hands-on experience with the product and that your opinions are well-founded. High-quality video demos, especially when posted on platforms like YouTube or integrated into blog posts, can set you apart from competitors.

For example, you might create a video where you walk through a specific task—such as generating a blog post outline using ChatGPT. As you demonstrate each step, provide commentary on the user interface, ease of integration with other tools, and the quality of the content produced. Combine this with a written review that summarizes key points, supplemented by screenshots and key data points.

Content Strategies for TikTok, YouTube, Blogs, and Newsletters

To successfully market AI tools through affiliate marketing, it's essential to diversify your content channels. Each platform offers unique advantages and caters to different audience preferences. Here's how you can strategize for each:

TikTok

TikTok is all about short, engaging video content. It's a powerful platform for reaching a wide, tech-savvy audience. To succeed on TikTok:

- **Create Bite-Sized Content:** Develop short tutorials and quick reviews that highlight key features or benefits of AI tools. Use attention-grabbing visuals and clear, concise messaging.
- **Trend Integration:** Leverage trending hashtags, challenges, and sound clips related to technology and AI. For instance, if there is a trending sound that can be repurposed to highlight a tool's efficiency, use it.
- **Demonstrate Use Cases:** Show the real-world application of AI tools in under a minute. A series where you demonstrate "AI Tips in 30 Seconds" for improving productivity can resonate well with busy professionals.
- **Engage with Viewers:** Encourage viewers to ask questions in the comments. Use these interactions for future content ideas, such as detailed review videos or Q&A sessions.

YouTube

YouTube is ideal for longer-form, in-depth content. Here's how to establish yourself on YouTube:

- **Detailed Reviews and Demos:** Produce 10- to 20-minute videos where you provide in-depth reviews, use-case demonstrations, and comparisons between different AI tools.
- **Tutorial Series:** Create a playlist focused on "Getting Started with AI Tools" that walks users through various applications—from setting up an account to integrating tools into daily workflows.
- **Live Sessions and Webinars:** Occasionally host live streams to interact with your audience in real time, answer questions, and delve into complex topics that require a deeper explanation.
- **High Production Quality:** Invest in good lighting, sound, and editing software. Well-produced videos build trust and make your content more shareable.
- **Calls to Action:** Include clear calls to action, encouraging viewers to check out affiliate links in the description, subscribe to your channel, and join your newsletter for updates.

Blogging

A blog is the backbone of your content marketing strategy, providing SEO value and a repository for detailed guides and reviews.

- **In-Depth Articles:** Write comprehensive posts that offer detailed reviews, comparisons, and tutorials. For example, "The Ultimate Guide to AI-Powered Writing Tools" could serve as a cornerstone piece.

- **SEO Optimization:** Use keyword research to identify terms your target audience is searching for. Optimize your posts with relevant keywords, metadata, and structured content to improve search engine rankings.
- **Visuals and Embedded Media:** Enhance your posts with screenshots, diagrams, and embedded videos from your YouTube channel. This creates an immersive experience that holds the reader's attention.
- **User Engagement:** Allow comments and encourage readers to share their experiences with the tools. This builds community and provides valuable feedback that you can leverage for future content.
- **Regular Updates:** Keep your blog content updated with the latest trends and tool updates. Regular posts help maintain and grow your organic audience over time.

Newsletters

Email newsletters are crucial for building a loyal audience base that you can monetize over the long term.

- **Curated Content:** Deliver a mix of your latest reviews, tips for using AI tools, and industry news. This keeps your subscribers informed and engaged.
- **Exclusive Insights:** Offer subscribers exclusive insights, downloadable guides, or early access to new content. This adds value to being on your mailing list.
- **Automation Integration:** Use email automation to segment

your audience based on interests, sending tailored content that resonates with different subscriber groups.

- **Conversion-Driven Campaigns:** Occasionally send out special offers, affiliate promotions, or invitations to webinars and live sessions. Be clear about how these resources can help your readers solve their challenges.

By leveraging each of these channels strategically, you can create a robust, multi-platform presence that drives traffic to your affiliate links and builds your authority in the AI niche.

Email Automation and Content at Scale

The power of email automation cannot be understated when it comes to scaling your content distribution and affiliate marketing efforts. It allows you to nurture leads, deliver personalized content, and drive conversions without constant manual effort.

Setting Up Automated Email Sequences

Start by setting up a series of automated emails that guide new subscribers through a journey:

- **Welcome Sequence:** Introduce yourself, explain your mission in the AI space, and set expectations about the type of content subscribers will receive. Offer a valuable free resource, such as a mini-guide or a video series.
- **Educational Sequence:** Over the next few emails, provide

educational content that explains key concepts related to AI tools, affiliate marketing, and the benefits of embracing AI technology in everyday business operations.

- **Review and Recommendation Sequence:** Gradually transition to content that focuses on detailed reviews and recommendations of AI tools. Use these emails to feature case studies, personal experiences, and success stories.
- **Promotion and Affiliate Offers:** Finally, include clear calls to action that encourage your subscribers to try the tools you've reviewed using your affiliate links. Make sure these emails highlight the benefits and offer clear instructions on how to get started.

Using AI to Personalize and Scale Content

Advanced email marketing platforms, such as Mailchimp, ConvertKit, or ActiveCampaign, now include AI-driven personalization features. These features analyze subscriber behavior and engagement metrics to automatically tailor content for each user:

- **Dynamic Content Blocks:** Use dynamic content blocks to serve different messages based on the subscriber's past interactions or demographic profile.
- **Behavioral Triggered Emails:** Automatically send targeted emails based on specific actions—like clicking a link, watching a video, or visiting a particular page on your website.
- **Content Suggestions:** AI can analyze the performance of past campaigns and suggest adjustments to subject lines, send times, or content format to optimize open and click-

through rates.

By integrating these AI-powered email automation techniques, you can ensure that your content is not only delivered at scale but also personalized to maximize engagement and conversion rates.

Becoming an Authority in an AI Niche

To succeed in affiliate marketing for AI tools, establishing yourself as an authority in a specific niche is key. When you are seen as a trusted expert, your recommendations carry more weight, and your audience is more likely to follow your guidance.

Building Expertise and Credibility

- **Deep Focus on a Sub-Niche:** Instead of trying to cover every AI tool available, select a specific area where you have both passion and knowledge. This could be AI-powered content creation, customer service automation, AI tools for small businesses, or any segment where you see both demand and a gap in quality content.
- **Consistent Content Creation:** Regularly produce high-quality content that addresses the needs and challenges of your target audience. This includes blog posts, videos, podcasts, and social media posts. Consistency reinforces your expertise and keeps your audience engaged.
- **Engage with the Community:** Participate in forums, com-

ment on industry blogs, join LinkedIn groups, and engage with social media communities related to your niche. Sharing your insights and responding to questions not only boosts your visibility but also helps refine your expertise through active dialogue.

- **Thought Leadership:** Contribute guest posts, appear in interviews, and participate in webinars or industry events. These activities help position you as a go-to resource for reliable information in your field.
- **Transparency in Reviews:** Build trust by being honest about the pros and cons of the AI tools you review. A balanced perspective that includes both strengths and weaknesses will resonate with your audience and establish you as a trustworthy voice.

Leveraging Social Proof

Social proof is critical when establishing authority. Encourage your audience to leave reviews, testimonials, and share their success stories with the tools you promote. Highlight positive feedback and case studies on your website and social media channels to showcase the real-world impact of your recommendations.

A Passive Income Playbook with AI Tools

The ultimate goal of affiliate marketing is not just to build authority, but to create a sustainable, passive income stream. Once you have set up your content channels, automated your outreach, and established your authority, the income generated through affiliate commissions can become a significant revenue source. Here's how to create a playbook for passive income with AI tools:

Monetizing Through Affiliate Links

- **Strategic Placement:** Integrate affiliate links naturally into your content. Whether in video descriptions, blog posts, emails, or social media posts, ensure the links are contextually relevant and provide clear value to the user.
- **Content Clusters:** Create content clusters around specific AI tools. For instance, a series of posts or videos dedicated to "Mastering AI for Content Creation" can funnel viewers toward affiliate links for AI writing and design tools.
- **Comparisons and Reviews:** Develop comprehensive comparison posts that highlight the benefits and drawbacks of multiple tools. These posts are particularly effective at driving affiliate conversions, as they help readers make informed decisions.
- **Incentivized Offers:** Occasionally, partner with AI platforms for exclusive discounts, free trials, or special promotions. Offering these incentives can boost click-through and conversion rates on your affiliate links.

Scaling Affiliate Revenue with Automation

- **Automated Content Creation:** Leverage AI to produce content at scale. Utilize tools like ChatGPT to generate drafts and ideas, then refine the content to ensure it meets your quality standards. More content means more opportunities to include affiliate links.

- **Email Campaigns:** As described earlier, use automated email sequences to promote your affiliate content. Regular, personalized emails keep your audience engaged and drive recurring clicks to affiliate offers.
- **Analytics and Optimization:** Use analytics tools to track affiliate performance. Identify which types of content and which channels generate the most revenue, then double down on those strategies. AI-powered analytics can provide insights into user behavior, helping you optimize your approach over time.

Diversification and Sustainability

Don't rely solely on one or two affiliate programs. Instead, diversify your income sources by partnering with multiple platforms that align with your niche. This approach reduces risk and ensures that changes in any single affiliate program won't significantly impact your overall revenue.

- **Content Monetization Platforms:** Consider integrating multiple monetization streams such as ad revenue from YouTube, sponsored posts on your blog, and affiliate marketing. This multi-channel approach spreads your risk and maximizes income potential.
- **Community Engagement:** Build a community around your content. Active engagement with your audience not only increases loyalty but also opens up opportunities for mentorships, consulting, or even developing your own AI tool—all of which can serve as additional revenue streams.

Case Studies and Real-Life Examples

Several successful affiliates have built sizable passive income streams by strategically promoting AI tools. For example, a content creator specializing in digital marketing might establish a blog dedicated to AI-powered marketing techniques, creating detailed guides and video tutorials. By integrating affiliate links to tools like ChatGPT, Canva, and various analytics platforms, they generate steady income from each piece of content. With regular updates, email nurturing, and active community engagement, such a platform can continue to grow its audience and revenue over time.

Becoming a Trusted Authority and Passive Income Catalyst

Ultimately, the key to success in affiliate marketing for AI tools is to become the trusted authority that your audience turns to for reliable, unbiased information. When your followers believe that your recommendations are based on thorough research and genuine experience, they are more likely to convert on your affiliate links, leading to sustainable passive income.

Focus on building a brand that stands for quality and reliability. Invest the time to refine your reviews, continuously update your content to reflect the latest trends, and engage authentically with your audience. Over time, this consistent approach will create a flywheel effect: as your authority grows, so will your audience, and as your audience grows, your passive income will scale accordingly.

Final Thoughts

Affiliate marketing for AI tools represents one of the most exciting and potentially lucrative opportunities in today's digital economy. By systematically reviewing, demoing, and promoting AI platforms through multiple channels such as TikTok, YouTube, blogs, and newsletters, you can establish yourself as a key influencer in the space. When coupled with email automation and content at scale, these efforts transform into a consistent, passive income playbook.

The journey requires commitment, creativity, and a willingness to adapt as the AI landscape evolves. Focus on genuine problem-solving, provide detailed and honest content, and remain adaptive to new trends. As you build your authority in your chosen AI niche, your voice will attract partnerships, loyal followers, and sustainable revenue streams—all while establishing you as an indispensable part of the modern technological revolution.

Embrace the challenge and excitement of affiliate marketing for AI tools. With a clear strategy, the right mix of content channels, and robust automation to scale your efforts, you're well-positioned to turn your passion for AI into a thriving, passive income business. Step forward, leverage your insights, and become the trusted advisor that businesses and consumers look to in the ever-evolving world of artificial intelligence.

10

Chapter 10: Experimentation Lab — 30-Day AI Hustle Challenge

In the dynamic world of AI-driven entrepreneurship, the fastest way to learn and succeed is by diving in headfirst. The 30-Day AI Hustle Challenge is designed to be a hands-on, experimental lab where you can test out different methods, strategies, and tools to generate income, streamline work processes, and explore innovative ideas. This chapter is your roadmap for a month-long journey of experimentation, complete with try-it-yourself challenges, ready-to-use templates, prompts, automation recipes, and systematic ways to track your progress, revenue, and growth. More than anything, it's an invitation to test, pivot, and double down on what works best for your unique situation.

The Value of Experimentation

Innovation rarely comes from theory alone—it is forged in the fire of practical application. The AI Hustle Challenge is about embracing a startup mindset: moving quickly, learning from real-world feedback, and iterating until you find the winning formula. Throughout the month, you'll be encouraged to step out of your comfort zone, try different approaches, and measure the outcomes. Whether you're exploring freelance services, affiliate marketing, e-commerce automation, content creation, or developing your own AI tools, constant experimentation will lead you to discover new opportunities and refine your strategies.

The challenge is structured so that each day or each week focuses on a particular aspect of your AI-driven hustle. Think of it as a series of mini-projects designed to help you develop skills, optimize processes, and ultimately build a sustainable income stream.

Try-It-Yourself Challenges for Each Method

The first step in this challenge is identifying which methods you want to experiment with. Here are some key areas you might consider testing over the 30 days, along with a sample challenge for each:

Freelancing with AI Tools

Challenge: Offer one AI-augmented service on a freelance platform such as Upwork or Fiverr.

- **Task:** Use ChatGPT or Jasper to produce a piece of content (like a blog post or copywriting piece) and integrate Grammarly for edits.
- **Goal:** Secure your first client by showcasing rapid turnaround and high-quality output.
- **Measurement:** Track the number of proposals sent, responses received, and if you secure a contract, the feedback provided.

AI-Powered Content Creation

Challenge: Produce and publish at least two pieces of content (one YouTube video and one blog post) centered around AI tools.

- **Task:** Use a combination of ChatGPT for scripting, Pictory or Descript for video editing, and Midjourney for generating creative visuals.
- **Goal:** Engage at least 50 viewers or readers and encourage them to subscribe or comment with their thoughts.
- **Measurement:** Monitor engagement metrics such as view counts, likes, comments, and website traffic.

E-Commerce and AI Automation

Challenge: Set up an automated dropshipping store or print-on-demand business utilizing AI for product research and description generation.

- **Task:** Use AI tools to generate product descriptions and images automatically, and integrate a chatbot for customer service using platforms like Zapier.
- **Goal:** Achieve your first sale or generate inquiries from potential buyers within the first week of launch.
- **Measurement:** Track website traffic, click-through rates on product pages, and the number of completed orders.

Affiliate Marketing for AI Tools

Challenge: Launch a series of short-form social media content pieces promoting AI tools through your affiliate links.

- **Task:** Create 5 TikTok videos, a detailed YouTube review, and a blog post about a specific AI tool, incorporating your affiliate links naturally in the content.
- **Goal:** Attract clicks that lead to engagement with the affiliate offers; aim for a measurable number of affiliate conversions.
- **Measurement:** Use affiliate tracking tools to monitor click-through rates, conversion rates, and revenue generated.

Building and Selling AI Tools or SaaS

Challenge: Develop a simple AI-powered web app using a no-code platform that addresses a specific problem you've identified.

- **Task:** Identify a pain point (for example, automating social media post generation), build a basic tool using platforms like Bubble or Microsoft PowerApps, and create a demo video showing its use.
- **Goal:** Gather feedback from at least 10 potential users or early adopters via surveys or direct interviews.
- **Measurement:** Track user engagement, sign-ups, and qualitative feedback regarding usability and potential improvements.

AI Consulting

Challenge: Offer a free initial AI audit for a small business to identify inefficiencies and propose automation opportunities.

- **Task:** Create a simple audit template, meet with a business owner (or a volunteer from your network), and deliver a brief report with actionable AI recommendations.
- **Goal:** Convert at least one free audit into a paid consulting project by demonstrating tangible value.
- **Measurement:** Evaluate the impact through follow-up meetings, client testimonials, and any subsequent contracts secured.

Templates, Prompts, and Automation Recipes

To streamline your experiments, here are some ready-to-use assets you can adapt for your own projects:

Content Creation Template

Blog Post Review Template:

- **Title:** Craft a captivating title that hints at the main benefit of the tool (e.g., "How [AI Tool] Can Transform Your Content Creation Process").
- **Introduction:** Briefly introduce the tool, its purpose, and its potential value.
- **Features and Benefits:** Provide a section highlighting key features, how they function, and the benefits users can expect.
- **Use Case Scenario:** Share a real-world example of the tool in action, complete with before-and-after comparisons.
- **Call to Action:** End with a clear call to action, inviting readers to try out the tool using your affiliate link.

Video Script Prompt: "Write a detailed 500-word script for a YouTube review of [AI Tool]. Begin with a strong hook explaining how the tool can save time and enhance creativity. Follow with an overview of its features, a live demo segment, and a personal testimonial of its benefits. Conclude with a call-to-action encouraging viewers to click the affiliate link in the description for an exclusive discount."

Automation Workflow Recipe

Email Drip Campaign Recipe:

- **Tool:** Mailchimp or ConvertKit
- **Sequence:**
- **Email 1 (Welcome):** Introduce yourself and the purpose of the series. Offer a free resource, such as "5 AI Tools to Boost Your Productivity."
- **Email 2 (Educational):** Explain the benefits of AI tools. Include a case study that demonstrates measurable improvements.
- **Email 3 (Review):** Provide a detailed review of one specific AI tool, with insights and personal experiences.
- **Email 4 (Promotion):** Highlight an exclusive affiliate offer, with a clear call-to-action to click your link.
- **Email 5 (Follow-Up):** Request feedback and encourage questions to foster engagement.
- **Automation Tip:** Use AI-powered segmentation to send personalized emails based on subscriber behavior (e.g., clicks on affiliate links).

Freelancer Proposal Template

Freelancing with AI Tools:

"Hello [Client Name],

I noticed that you're looking for efficient ways to streamline your content creation. I specialize in leveraging AI tools like ChatGPT and Jasper to generate high-quality content quickly and efficiently. I can deliver fully edited and proofread content within [X] days, ensuring consistency and engagement for your target audience. Please find attached my portfolio and some case studies that highlight the results I've achieved for similar clients. I'm excited about the possibility of working with you to enhance your content strategy.

Best regards,

[Your Name]"

Tracking Progress, Revenue, and Growth

The success of the 30-Day AI Hustle Challenge relies on diligent tracking and analysis. Without clear metrics, it's impossible to know which experiments are working and which need to be pivoted. Here are some methods for tracking your progress:

Setting Key Performance Indicators (KPIs)

Establish clear KPIs for each experiment. Examples include:

- **Engagement Metrics:** For content creation, monitor video views, social media interactions, blog comments, and email open rates.
- **Conversion Rates:** For freelance services or affiliate links, track the number of inquiries, proposals accepted, and affiliate sales generated.
- **Revenue Tracking:** Use accounting tools or simple spreadsheets to log income from various streams—freelance projects, affiliate commissions, and SaaS subscriptions.
- **Time Efficiency:** Track how long tasks take before and after automation to measure productivity gains.

Tools for Monitoring and Analytics

- **Google Analytics:** Use this to track website traffic, conversion rates, and user behavior on your blog or e-commerce site.
- **Social Media Analytics:** Most social platforms provide detailed metrics on engagement, reach, and viewer demographics.
- **Affiliate Dashboard Tools:** Platforms like Amazon Associates or other affiliate programs offer built-in reporting dashboards that show clicks, conversions, and revenue.
- **Project Management Software:** Tools like Trello, Asana, or Notion can help you manage tasks, track progress, and set reminders for review and iteration.

Setting Up Regular Check-Ins

Create a schedule for regular review sessions. This could be weekly or bi-weekly check-ins where you analyze data, review what's working, and determine next steps. Document your findings and adjust your strategies as needed. This methodical approach ensures that you can pivot quickly if a particular experiment isn't generating the desired results.

Encouragement to Test, Pivot, and Double Down

The heart of the 30-Day AI Hustle Challenge is an experimental mindset. Not every idea will be an immediate success, and that's perfectly okay. The goal is to learn as much as possible in a short period, then double down on the strategies that show promise.

- **Embrace Failure:** Every setback is an opportunity to learn. If a particular marketing channel or approach isn't working, analyze the data to understand why and pivot accordingly.
- **Iterate Rapidly:** Use the data from your tracking tools to refine your tactics. Small improvements can compound over time, leading to significant gains.
- **Double Down on Success:** When you identify a strategy that works, focus more resources on it. This might mean increasing your content output, investing more time in a particular niche, or scaling up paid advertising on the platforms showing the best results.
- **Stay Agile:** The landscape of AI and digital marketing is constantly evolving. Be prepared to adjust your methods as new tools and trends emerge. Regularly update your templates, prompts, and automation workflows to reflect the latest best practices and tools.
- **Community Feedback:** Engage with your peers and mentors in the AI and digital marketing communities. Share your progress, ask for advice, and be open to feedback. This network can provide valuable insights and support as you refine your strategies.

Wrapping Up the 30-Day Challenge

By the end of the 30 days, you should have a comprehensive set of data points, insights, and new skills that form the foundation for your AI-driven hustle. The experimentation lab should yield:

- A portfolio of content across multiple channels (videos, blog posts, social media snippets, etc.) that demonstrates your ability to produce and promote engaging material.
- A collection of client proposals, case studies, and potentially a few initial contracts or affiliate sales that validate your market approach.
- A refined set of workflows and automation recipes that streamline your operations and increase efficiency.
- Clear metrics that show growth in revenue, engagement, and overall performance.

Remember that this challenge is only the beginning. The insights and momentum gained during these 30 days can serve as a springboard for larger projects, new services, or even a full-scale AI consultancy. Your ability to adapt, learn, and optimize will be the true differentiator in a competitive landscape.

Final Thoughts and Next Steps

The 30-Day AI Hustle Challenge is your call to action—a structured but flexible plan designed to push you out of your comfort zone and into the reality of building a sustainable AI-driven venture. Throughout this chapter, you've seen how to approach various methods, from freelancing and content creation to e-commerce, affiliate marketing, and beyond. Now, armed with templates, automation recipes, and a robust framework for tracking your progress, you are ready to dive into experimentation.

Your next steps should be:

- Commit to the challenge by blocking off time each day to work on your experiments.
- Set up your tracking dashboards and define your KPIs clearly.
- Utilize the provided templates and prompts to streamline your initial efforts.
- Schedule regular review sessions to assess progress and make adjustments.
- Engage with your community to share insights, troubleshoot challenges, and celebrate successes.

Innovation and success in the digital age are driven by action. The challenge encourages you to test boldly, learn relentlessly, and pivot when necessary. By embracing this iterative process and focusing on actionable data, you can transform experimental ideas into reliable income streams.

As you complete the 30 days, reflect on your progress, refine your strategies, and prepare to double down on what works best. With commitment, agility, and the continuous drive to improve, the 30-Day AI Hustle Challenge can be the catalyst for your future success in the world of AI-driven entrepreneurship.

Step into the experimentation lab with confidence, knowing that each challenge, each iteration, and each pivot is paving the way to a profitable and scalable future. Embrace the journey, celebrate your learnings, and let the data guide you toward sustained growth and opportunity.

Welcome to the 30-Day AI Hustle Challenge—your laboratory for innovation, your training ground for entrepreneurship, and your pathway to turning ideas into thriving, passive income ventures. Now is the time to test, learn, and transform your hustle into reality.

11

Conclusion

The Gold Rush Mindset

As we reach the end of this journey, it's time to step back and reflect on what the AI Gold Rush truly represents—not only as a series of practical strategies for generating income and innovating with technology, but also as a mindset. The essence of the Gold Rush Mindset goes beyond the excitement of rapid gains or overnight successes; it is rooted in sustainability, continuous learning, and a commitment to building long-term value. In an era where hype and short-term tactics are often glorified, the real reward lies in forging a path that remains resilient and adaptive over time.

The AI landscape is brimming with possibilities, and it's easy to be swept away by buzzwords and the allure of fast money. Hype can be intoxicating, promising quick fixes and instant breakthroughs. In many industries, particularly one as dynamic and transformative as artificial intelligence, temporary spikes in enthusiasm often lead to fleeting trends. The temptation to jump on every shiny new tool or strategy is strong, but it is essential to look past the flashy promises and focus on building something that stands the test of time. True success in the AI Gold Rush is measured by what you create and how it endures, not by momentary virality.

Sustainability versus Hype

It is easy to get caught up in a culture that celebrates short-term wins. Social media platforms, for example, are inundated with testimonials of explosive growth and overnight success stories. But these narratives, while inspirational, often overlook the amount of hard work, failures, and strategic pivots that paved the way for lasting achievements. The risk in following hype is that you might invest your time and energy in projects that yield rapid results initially but ultimately do not create value in the long run.

In contrast, a sustainable approach is one where every decision is measured against the benchmark of long-term viability. When you evaluate an AI strategy, think not only about the immediate gains but also about whether it will contribute to your growth five or ten years down the road. A sustainable project is built on robust foundations, designed with scalability in mind, and continuously refined to meet evolving market demands. While hyperbolic claims and rapid returns may sound exciting, the most rewarding ventures are those that endure beyond the fleeting moments of hype.

Focus on Long-Term Value, Not Short-Term Hacks

Embracing the long-term perspective requires a shift in mindset—from seeking quick fixes to investing in ideas, skills, and systems that deliver value over time. The temptation to rely on shortcuts and opportunistic hacks is strong, but such approaches are often unsustainable. Instead, successful entrepreneurs understand that building lasting success requires deliberate planning, sustained effort, and an unwavering focus on quality.

Take, for example, the rapid, short-lived spikes often seen in social media trends. These may provide a temporary boost in engagement, but without a deeper strategy that connects with your audience's needs, they will eventually fade away. In the realm of AI, it's essential to ask: Does this new tool or tactic truly improve efficiency, enhance customer experience, or drive innovation in a meaningful way? If the answer isn't clear, it may be wiser to hold off rather than chasing the next big thing.

Prioritizing long-term value also means investing in your own knowledge and capabilities. The AI landscape is constantly evolving, and what works today may be obsolete tomorrow. Therefore, the true asset you have is your ability to learn and adapt—a quality that will enable you to navigate change and turn new challenges into opportunities. Every project, every experiment, and every setback is a step toward greater expertise. By focusing on strategies that accumulate value over time, you build a foundation that not only supports your current efforts but also opens doors to new ventures and opportunities in the future.

Continue Learning and Adapting with AI

One of the most exciting aspects of working with artificial intelligence is its relentless pace of innovation. New algorithms, platforms, and tools emerge regularly, and the potential applications of AI continue to expand at a breathtaking rate. This constant state of flux demands that you, as an entrepreneur or professional, remain agile and committed to continuous learning.

Investing in education and skill development is not merely an option; it is a necessity in this field. Whether you are reading industry reports, participating in online courses, attending webinars, or following thought leaders on social media, staying informed is critical. There is a wealth of knowledge available, and by continuously seeking it out, you ensure that you remain at the cutting edge of technology and market trends.

Moreover, as you integrate AI into your business processes, you will encounter both successes and failures. Each failure is not a sign to give up, but rather a valuable learning opportunity—a chance to analyze what went wrong, understand the underlying challenges, and refine your approach. The iterative process of testing, failing, and iterating is at the heart of innovation. Embrace it as part of your journey.

Adaptability is equally important. As markets evolve and new competitors emerge, the strategies and tools that once brought success may need to be reimagined. Being open to change and willing to pivot is what separates enduring ventures from those that falter under pressure. Keep your finger on the pulse of technological advancements and market trends. Look for ways to integrate new discoveries into your existing workflows and never shy away from experimenting with novel ideas—even if they seem untested at first.

The key is not to be paralyzed by uncertainty but to see it as a dynamic environment where opportunities abound for those who are prepared to seize them. Your ability to adapt will be your greatest asset, enabling you to stay ahead of the curve and turn emerging trends into sustained growth.

Final Encouragement to Act, Experiment, and Build

As you conclude this journey through the AI Gold Rush, remember that the future belongs to those who take initiative. The strategies, tools, and insights presented in this book are not mere theoretical concepts; they are practical, actionable steps that have the potential to reshape your professional life. Yet, knowing and understanding these strategies is only half the battle—the other half lies in taking action.

Now is the time to step out of your comfort zone and start experimenting. Embrace a mindset of continuous trial and improvement. Every project you undertake, every tool you test, and every campaign you launch is a building block toward a larger, more resilient enterprise. The most important thing is to get started. Don't wait for the perfect moment or for all uncertainties to vanish; perfect conditions rarely exist in the real world. Instead, commit to taking small, deliberate steps every day that move you toward your larger goals.

Act with courage and determination. In the rapidly evolving field of AI, opportunities are fleeting, and the competitive landscape is unforgiving. Each day that you delay is a missed chance to learn, to innovate, and to establish yourself as a leader in your niche. And remember, even if some experiments do not yield the expected results, every experience provides valuable lessons. What appears to be a failure on the surface may well be the catalyst for a breakthrough if you are willing to analyze, adapt, and refine your approach.

Build a mindset that is both resilient and ambitious. While it is important to manage risk and stay grounded, do not allow fear of failure to inhibit your progress. The AI revolution is inherently experimental, and those who are bold enough to explore uncharted territories will often reap substantial rewards. Continue to seek out opportunities for growth, whether through new projects, partnerships, or by venturing into untested markets. The key is to remain proactive and resourceful, continually iterating on your ideas until you find what truly works.

Focus on the long-term vision rather than short-term gains. The Gold Rush Mindset is not about chasing fleeting trends or quick wins—it is about laying a foundation for enduring success.

Prioritize projects and strategies that add real value, both for your business and for your customers. Align your efforts with broader goals that transcend immediate profit, such as innovation, customer satisfaction, and sustained competitive advantage. This long-term perspective is what will ultimately drive lasting impact and ensure that your entrepreneurial journey is both profitable and fulfilling.

In addition, build a network of like-minded individuals. Surround yourself with fellow entrepreneurs, innovators, and mentors who share your passion for AI and can provide guidance, feedback, and support. Collaboration is a powerful catalyst for growth. Engage with communities, participate in forums, and attend industry events. By exchanging ideas and experiences, you expand your horizon, gain new insights, and reinforce your commitment to continuous learning and adaptation.

As you move forward, keep your focus on both the big picture and the fine details. Celebrate small victories along the way— they are the stepping stones to more significant achievements. Maintain a detailed record of your experiments, outcomes, and lessons learned. This documentation will serve as both a roadmap for your progress and a reminder of how far you have come. Use it to refine your strategies and to inspire yourself when challenges arise.

Above all, remember that the journey is as important as the destination. The process of building, experimenting, and learning is where the true value lies. Embrace every opportunity as a chance to grow, and never underestimate the power of persistence. The AI Gold Rush is not reserved for those who wait for perfect conditions but for those who take decisive, informed actions and continuously push the boundaries of what is possible.

In conclusion, adopting the Gold Rush Mindset means committing to sustainability over hype, focusing on long-term value rather than quick fixes, and embracing a perpetual cycle of learning and adaptation. It requires bold actions, the willingness to experiment, and the determination to build something enduring despite uncertainties. As you embark on your next chapter—whether launching a new venture, scaling your business, or simply integrating AI into your daily operations—carry with you the conviction that every step you take is a stride toward success.

Now is the moment to act. Experiment boldly, learn relentlessly, and build a future that is not only profitable but also resilient and innovative. Let the spirit of the Gold Rush guide you to uncover hidden opportunities, refine your approach, and construct a legacy that stands as a testament to your vision and perseverance. Step forward with confidence, and transform the power of AI into a thriving reality.

Appendix

AI Tools Directory

Generative AI Tools

- **ChatGPT:** A conversational AI that helps generate written content, offers brainstorming assistance, and supports ideation across various industries.
- **Jasper:** Tailored for marketing copy and long-form content, Jasper streamlines creative writing and optimizes output for SEO.
- **Claude:** An alternative LLM known for its clear summarizations and insightful content generation.
- **Sudowrite:** An AI tool that assists creative writers to expand, rephrase, and polish drafts, ideal for overcoming writer's block.

Visual and Multimedia AI Tools

- **Canva:** A user-friendly design platform enhanced with AI-powered suggestions for creating visuals, infographics, and social media content.
- **Midjourney:** Generates AI-created artwork and mood boards, useful for visual branding and creative concepting.

- **Pictory:** A video editing solution that transforms long-form content into short, engaging clips ideal for social media.

Automation and Integration Tools

- **Zapier:** Connects various applications and automates workflows, reducing repetitive tasks without coding.
- **Make (formerly Integromat):** Similar to Zapier, it offers deeper integrations and visual workflow automation to streamline processes.
- **Microsoft PowerApps:** A low-code platform to build business apps that integrate with other Microsoft services.
- **Analytics and Trading Tools**
- **Trade Ideas:** Provides AI-driven stock screening and predictive analytics to help identify high-probability trading opportunities.
- **QuantConnect:** A platform for developing, backtesting, and deploying quantitative trading strategies using AI.

Recommended Resources

Courses:

- *AI For Everyone* (Coursera): An accessible overview of AI concepts and their practical applications for all business types.
- *Machine Learning Specialization* (Coursera/Udacity): In-depth courses covering algorithms, data science, and the practical implementation of machine learning models.
- *No-Code Development* (Udemy): Courses focusing on lever-

aging no-code and low-code platforms for app development.

Newsletters:

- *The Algorithm* by MIT Technology Review: Regular insights into AI trends and technological breakthroughs.
- *Import AI:* Curated updates and analysis from the world of artificial intelligence.
- *Ben Evans' Newsletter:* Strategic analysis and thought leadership covering technology and market trends.

Communities:

- *Reddit r/MachineLearning:* Discussions, research updates, and community-driven advice on machine learning.
- *Hacker News:* A forum for sharing and debating the latest tech news, including AI developments.
- *AI Alignment Forum:* A specialized community for deeper discussions on AI safety, ethics, and long-term impacts.

Prompt Library for Different Use Cases

Writing:

- "Generate a detailed blog post outline on [Topic] that includes an introduction, key points, and a conclusion."
- "Write a creative short story set in the future where AI plays a central role in everyday life."
- "Summarize the latest trends in AI research and explain their potential implications for small businesses."

Video Creation:

- "Draft a 5-minute script for a YouTube video reviewing the top 3 AI tools for content creation."
- "Write a storyboard for a TikTok video that demonstrates a quick tip using an AI tool for digital marketing."
- "Generate a video outline that explains how to integrate Zapier into a simple automation workflow."

Sales and Marketing:

- "Create a persuasive email copy promoting [AI Tool], emphasizing its key benefits and ROI for small businesses."
- "Draft ad copy for a social media campaign focused on an exclusive discount for new users of [AI Platform]."
- "Generate a product description for [AI Tool] that highlights its unique features and integrates relevant SEO keywords."

General Productivity:

- "Write an outline for a webinar on leveraging AI for productivity enhancement in modern workplaces."
- "Generate bullet points for a presentation on how AI can automate routine business processes."

Productivity Stack Templates

Notion:

- *Project Management Dashboard:* A customizable template to track tasks, set deadlines, and manage client projects with integrated progress bars and KPIs.

- *Content Calendar:* A template that allows you to plan, schedule, and collaborate on content creation, complete with sections for idea generation, drafting, and publishing.

Trello:

- *Kanban Board for Workflows:* A simple board with columns for Backlog, In Progress, Review, and Completed tasks, ideal for managing projects and tracking progress with visual cues.
- *Editorial Calendar:* A template with cards for each piece of content, set with deadlines, assignees, and status updates to streamline content production workflows.

Airtable:

- *Content Production Tracker:* A database template designed to manage content pipelines, assign tasks, and monitor performance metrics with customizable fields for product details, deadlines, and performance data.
- *Client Project Management:* An Airtable base to track client projects, progress, milestones, and deliverables, integrating seamlessly with calendars and file attachments for a centralized overview.

About the Author

Andrew Davis is an automation strategist with over 15 years of experience helping businesses streamline operations and scale with technology. A lifelong tech enthusiast, Andrew is passionate about the transformative power of artificial intelligence and its potential to unlock new opportunities for entrepreneurs, creators, and professionals alike. Through his writing and work, he aims to make cutting-edge tools accessible and actionable, empowering others to embrace the AI-driven future with confidence and clarity.

www.ingramcontent.com/pod-product-compliance
Lightning Source LLC
LaVergne TN
LVHW051334050326
832903LV00031B/3535